Thi

REFLECTIONS
ON
BEHAVIORISM
AND
SOCIETY

REFLECTIONS
ON
BEHAVIORISM
AND
SOCIETY

B. F. Skinner

PRENTICE-HALL, INC., *Englewood Cliffs, N.J. 07632*

Library of Congress Cataloging in Publication Data

SKINNER, BURRHUS FREDERIC,
    Reflections on behaviorism and society.

    Includes bibliographical references and index.
    1. Behaviorism.   2. Personality and culture.
I. Title.
BF199.S55   301.1   77-28636
    ISBN 0-13-770057-1

Printed in the United States of America

10 9 8 7 6 5 4 3 2 1

PRENTICE-HALL INTERNATIONAL, INC., *London*
PRENTICE-HALL OF AUSTRALIA PTY. LIMITED, *Sydney*
PRENTICE-HALL OF CANADA, LTD., *Toronto*
PRENTICE-HALL OF INDIA PRIVATE LIMITED, *New Delhi*
PRENTICE-HALL OF JAPAN, INC., *Tokyo*
PRENTICE-HALL OF SOUTHEAST ASIA PTE. LTD., *Singapore*
WHITEHALL BOOKS LIMITED, *Wellington, New Zealand*

To
Eve *renée*

Contents

Preface

I   SOCIETY

1   Human Behavior and Democracy   3

2   Are We Free to Have a Future?   16

3   The Ethics of Helping People   33

4   Humanism and Behaviorism   48

5   Walden Two Revisited · 56

II   THE SCIENCE OF BEHAVIOR

6   The Steep and Thorny Way to a
Science of Behavior   68

7   Can We Profit from Our Discovery of
Behavioral Science?   83

8   Why I Am Not a Cognitive Psychologist   97

9   The Experimental Analysis of Behavior (A History)   113

III EDUCATION

10 Some Implications of Making Education More Efficient   *129*

11 The Free and Happy Student   *140*

12 Designing Higher Education   *149*

IV A MISCELLANY

13 The Shaping of Phylogenic Behavior   *163*

14 The Force of Coincidence   *169*

15 Reflections on Meaning and Structure   *176*

16 Walden (One) and Walden Two   *188*

17 Freedom and Dignity Revisited   *195*

18 Freedom at Last, from the Burden of Taxation   *199*

Acknowledgments   *202*

Index   *205*

Preface

This is not a book to be read straight through. Most of the papers were occasional, and the occasions various. For those who prefer an overview, here is a brief synopsis:

1. Behavior modification is just the technology we need to promote the face-to-face control of people, by people, and for people and thus to reduce the scope of the centralized institutions of government and economics.

2. We are beginning to be seriously concerned about the future. How can people be induced to behave in ways that take the future into account? There are relevant behavioral processes, but only the most careful planning will enable us to use them to solve our problems.

3. The things we call "good" work for our good, or for the good of others, only when they are usefully contingent on behavior. We do not really help others simply by giving them good things.

4. It is a mistake to identify humanism with the self-centered individualism of the existentialists. By identifying the role of the environment, particularly the social

environment, behaviorism makes it possible to achieve the goals of humanism more effectively.

5. *Walden Two* is more relevant today than when it was written thirty-two years ago. It describes a minimally consuming, minimally polluting, maximally socializing culture. It is not a bad start toward restoring the place of small communities in modern life.

6. The major obstacles to progress in a science of behavior are certain long-standing commitments to an inner world of the individual, either the metaphorical world of the mentalistic or cognitive psychologist or the real but not at the moment relevant world of the physiologist.

7. The effective management of human behavior is jeopardized when we appeal to feelings and ideas in the explanation of behavior. In doing so we neglect useful environmental contingencies.

8. Cognitive psychologists engage in a metaphorical translocation of the environment, moving contingencies of reinforcement, severally or as a whole, into the supposed world of the mind. It is assumed that people can somehow adjust to private contingencies more effectively because of the intimacy.
But the changes in behavior attributed to the supposed internal contingencies are due instead to the external contingencies from which they were derived.

9. (A brief account of the author's part in the evolution of the experimental analysis of behavior.)

10. The experimental analysis of behavior has improved education by clarifying its objectives, suggesting new practices in classroom management, and introducing instructional programming texts and other materials. As a result students learn in less time and with less effort, but difficult problems are then raised for the educational establishment.

11. Rousseau's free and happy student appears to be neither free nor happy. Permissiveness is not the only alternative to the aversive control characteristic of education throughout its history. Other feasible alternatives make it possible to prepare young people for the future that lies ahead of them.

12. Teachers who leave education to the innate curiosity of the student in a natural "learning environment" abandon their role as transmitters of the culture. New instruc-

tional practices can restore that essential function. Higher education is especially resistant to a behavioral technology, but changes are being made—as in the personalized system of instruction of F. S. Keller.

13. It is possible that instinctive behavior has been "shaped" by a process of selection not unlike the shaping of the behavior of the individual, although it required hundreds of millions of years rather than hundreds of seconds. Recent discoveries in the field of plate tectonics or "continental drift" point to slow changes in the environment which may have shaped some unusual examples of species behavior.

14. Certain kinds of coincidences are often said to show an underlying order in the world that has not been recognized by science. It is easy to collect instances, not because they are common, but because they are particularly likely to be noted and remembered. Coincidences attract our attention in part because the relation between response and consequence in operant conditioning is essentially coincidental.

15. Structuralism in linguistic and literary criticism does not yield a satisfactory analysis. We do not have the kinds of information about the writer needed for a convincing functional alternative, but internal relations among the parts of what a person writes sometimes point to relevant verbal processes.

16. *Walden Two* is not as different from Thoreau's *Walden (One)* as critics have claimed. Both books argue that we should examine the way of life into which we are born and if possible replace it with a better way. Both point to the advantages of simplifying one's life, and neither is escapist in any real sense. Young people today are discovering not only how they can simplify their lives but how they can solve a problem that Thoreau neglected—the problem of community.

17. By predicting that man would deliberately go mad to prove that his behavior could not be predicted, Dostoevsky cut off that last line of escape, because going mad was henceforth a predictable reaction. He thus illustrated one of the great paradoxes of freedom: any attempt to prove that man is free is probably less productive than changing our cultural practices in such a way that people feel freer than they have ever felt before. The change, nevertheless, implies a certain measure of control.

18. "State lotteries can become an ideal way in which free, happy, and affluent people support their government without paying taxes."

There is more in each chapter than I have been able to put in a few sentences, as I trust the reader who now turns to parts that may be of interest will discover.

B. F. SKINNER

REFLECTIONS
ON
BEHAVIORISM
AND
SOCIETY

PART I

SOCIETY

1   *Human Behavior and Democracy*

2   *Are We Free to Have a Future?*

3   *The Ethics of Helping People*

4   *Humanism and Behaviorism*

5   *Walden Two Revisited*

I

Human Behavior
and Democracy

. . . That this nation, under God, shall have a new birth of freedom; and that control of the people, by the people, and for the people, shall not perish from the earth.

Abraham Lincoln? Not exactly. Lincoln said "government of the people," not "control," and there is a difference. To govern once meant simply to guide, but the word soon acquired a stronger meaning. Governments "compel obedience to authority." In other words, they treat people aversively—punishing them when they behave badly and relaxing a threat of punishment when they behave well.

When they are too aversive, people escape from them or attack and weaken them with violence, terrorism, protests, strikes, boycotts, or revolution. They thus impose a kind of countercontrol upon the power to punish. Some sort of equilibrium may be reached, and we then speak of government "by the consent of the governed," where "consent" marks the limit beyond which an authority may not compel obedience. Note that the countercontrol, like the control, is aversive. The presumed value of a "government by the people" is that when people govern themselves they will use aversive measures with restraint.

But why should governments confine themselves to aversive control? Why not use positive reinforcement? Many governments have the means of doing so; they have the power to provide as well as punish. One answer may be that positive reinforcement is not well understood. Its effects are easily overlooked; we do not feel the control exerted when our own behavior is positively reinforced. Aversive action also has a kind of genetic priority. Aggressive repertoires, as well as the capacity to acquire aggressive behavior readily, have had survival value. It is also easy to learn to treat others aversively because the results are especially quick. Nevertheless, negative reinforcement and punishment have serious disadvantages which deserve attention, particularly now that democracy as a philosophy of government is in trouble. There are only a few real democracies in the world today, and the demise of democratic government is being widely predicted. Emerging nations tend to adopt the pattern of obedience to authority, epitomized in the military dictatorship, and many older nations are moving in that direction. Simply as the aversive countercontrol of the power to treat people aversively, democracy is losing ground. Can we save it, and preserve and further its achievements, by making a greater use of nonaversive measures?

It may be argued that something of the sort is done in the welfare state. Our own government is perhaps as much concerned with freedom from want as with freedom from fear; consider the services it provides in health, education, and welfare. Britain and the Scandinavian countries have gone much further, of course, and so, at least in theory, have the communist countries. But it is hard to find positive reinforcement in any of this. Welfare states sustain themselves with aversive practices. They acquire the goods they distribute through taxation (backed by a threat of punishment) or through the coercion of labor, and if they distribute goods "according to need" it is largely according to whether the needy will otherwise protest. The welfare or communist state also shows an unstable equilibrium between aversive control and countercontrol.

Moreover, and this is the important point, it does not make the goods it distributes contingent upon the behavior of its citizens. It does not use them as reinforcers but as appeasement, to reduce countercontrolling action. At best it moderates certain conditions that may otherwise lead to punishable behavior, since people are presumably more likely to behave well in a world free of poverty, illness, unemployment, and ignorance. But even full-fledged welfare states continue to punish misbehavior, and strong punitive sanctions certainly survive in communist countries.

We cannot avoid the conclusion that something that could contribute to government in the broadest sense is being overlooked. Positive reinforcement, as the term implies, is strengthening. It lacks both the suppressive and the aggressive effects of punishment, and it is free of the effects of negative reinforcement that we associate with anxiety and fear. Positively reinforced behavior is active participation in life, free of boredom and depression. When our behavior is positively reinforced we say we enjoy what we are doing; we call ourselves happy. Certainly these features of human behavior should be among the goals of any government "for the people," but they are out of reach of governments which merely compel obedience and are, at best, left to chance in welfare states. Can they be brought within reach in a democracy?

Let us look at two problems faced by all forms of government in the world today but especially relevant here because they have been created by what would certainly be regarded as the two great triumphs of a democratic way of life. Significantly, they are also the products of the basic behavioral processes we are considering. To borrow an expression which is perhaps too familiar, the ways in which people react to negative and positive reinforcement have led to the establishment of the rights to life and liberty and to the pursuit of happiness, respectively. They have also led to trouble. No matter how essential to the survival of a species a process may once have been, it can become troublesome or even lethal when the environment changes, and this has happened to both positive and negative reinforcement.

The processes through which organisms learn to escape from

or avoid various kinds of physical damage have had an obvious survival value, but in what we call a civilized environment they become less important, and a point may be reached at which they work against survival. For example, a vast technology has been developed to prevent, reduce, or terminate exhausting labor and physical damage. It is now dedicated to the production of the most trivial conveniences and comfort. Not only do we not suffer extremes of cold and heat, we keep our buildings within a narrow range of temperatures. Not only do we not work to near exhaustion, we ride escalators rather than climb stairs and push buttons to open the windows of our cars. Unless we then devise strenuous and stressful substitutes, we find ourselves vulnerable to any strong environmental demand, as well as to stronger people (the archetypal pattern of the civilized person versus the barbarian). Moreover, because the technology cannot be made available to everyone, our trivial gains mean costly losses for others.

The social parallel is far more important. No one will question the importance of the historical struggle for freedom, through which people have escaped from and weakened or destroyed those who have treated them aversively, but this process of establishing the right to life and liberty has reached the point at which *any* infringement upon the free movement of the individual is challenged. People claim the right to do as they please—to gamble away a fortune, risk unnecessary danger by not wearing a seat belt, die an alcoholic, and consume resources and pollute the environment without restriction. Students are to enjoy free and open classrooms, people with problems are not to be told what to do but are to find solutions within themselves, business is to flourish in an atmosphere of laissez-faire, and the form of behavior most subject to complaint by one's peers is complaint itself.

It is perhaps a natural mistake to suppose that the abolition of aversive social control leads in the end to this kind of permissiveness but, like convenience and comfort, small personal freedoms are purchased at great social cost. Everyone suffers when people are ill-mannered, illiterate, and ignorant, when laws are frequently broken, when people continue to need help, when goods are unequally distributed, and when so-called victimless crimes prove to have victims. In short, the world has changed, and the processes through which we free ourselves from aversive stimulation, nonsocial and social, have begun to work against the survival of the culture and possibly the species.

There has been a comparable miscarriage of the process of positive reinforcement. Jefferson borrowed the phrase "the pursuit of happiness" from John Locke, but Locke had said "the pursuit of property." The technology now devoted to the production of reinforcing goods is far more extensive than that concerned with the avoidance of exhausting labor and physical damage, and unless it is restrained it will soon exhaust the world's resources. It has another serious effect because people differ in the ability to acquire property and hence in the quantities they possess, and since possession usually makes acquisition easier, differences have become very great. Positive reinforcement has led not only to great wealth but to extreme poverty. When the poor become numerous enough or otherwise powerful enough to protest, they may be given some share of the wealth, but that leads to further trouble. Welfare—either as a social measure or as a political philosophy— raises the problem of the noncontingent reinforcer, to which I shall return.

Here, then, are two basic issues faced by all modern governments. Somewhere between freedom and despotism and between affluence and poverty there are points at which personal and social gains are balanced, but how can those points be reached? The most likely answer shows the traditional preoccupation with aversive control: we should enforce the laws, limit the extent to which people can acquire goods (as by taxing excesses), and make people work for what they get. But are there nonpunitive alternatives? Can we design an environment in which people will treat each other well, keep the size of the population within bounds, learn to work and work productively, preserve and enhance the reinforcing character of the world, explore and analyze that world, limit the use of resources and keep the environment safe for future generations, and do all this because the results are positively reinforcing?

A social environment in which people thus behave as they *like*, rather than as they *have*, to behave, has been the dream of many political and social reformers, but it is usually called "utopian" in the pejorative sense of impossible. Nevertheless, we are already under way in developing just such an alternative to government as the power to compel obedience. And it may lead to something that is closer to a government *of people by people* than anything yet proposed in the name of democracy.

People are governed, in the broadest sense, by the world in which they live, particularly by their social environments. The operation of such an environment is most obvious in a small homogeneous group, where behavior injurious to others is punished and behavior favoring others is reinforced, either by relaxing a threat or by presenting goods. As a social environment evolves, supportive practices appear. The group classifies behavior as good, bad, right, and wrong and uses these terms as conditioned reinforcers in strengthening or suppressing behavior. It describes some of the more important contingencies in the form of rules, and by following rules its members conform more quickly and avoid direct exposure to punitive consequences. Individuals may act to maintain the very contingencies to which they conform and when they do so without supervision, they are said to show self-control or the possession of an ethical or moral sense. Such a social environment transmits itself as new members of a group acquire the behavior of maintaining the contingencies.

Unfortunately, people govern people in this rather idealistic sense only when everyone has essentially the same power, and this is almost never the case. Someone emerges as a leader and, unfortunately, almost always by exerting a special share of the power to compel obedience. Countercontrol may limit that power, but the result is not a truly egalitarian society. Something of the same sort follows when a group delegates control to representatives, since delegation can have the same effect as usurpation. Preventing the misuse of power by one's own representatives is only a milder form of the struggle for freedom from tyranny. Neither process guarantees a balanced government.

It was once the practice to divide the social environment into three parts: (1) the polity (government in the narrow sense, specializing in aversive control), (2) the economy (specializing in the production and exchange of reinforcing goods), and (3) the culture, or all the other contingencies of reinforcement maintained by the group—in family practices, religious rituals, arts, crafts, and so on.

It is probably impossible to keep these fields apart, and in its modern use the term culture covers them all. A culture is a complete social environment, in which some contingencies are maintained by individuals and others by institutions. The earlier division was useful, however, because culture in the older sense meant the social contingencies not maintained by centralized agencies. Democracy has a special meaning when we apply the term to a culture in that sense.

It is then more obvious that control rests with the people. A social environment exists only because of what people do for and to other people, and it is never more than that even when power is usurped by, or delegated to, a special agency, but in a culture in the older sense the control is direct. Concentration of power in an agency is objectionable not only because it is characteristically misused and wasted but because it destroys interpersonal contacts. If I work for a company manufacturing shoes and my neighbor for a company manufacturing shirts, and if we both earn enough so that I buy a shirt and he or she a pair of shoes, we have in a sense produced something of value for each other, but there has been no direct exchange. A special opportunity to reinforce each other's behavior has been lost. Companies are no doubt needed for the efficient production of shoes and shirts, and we must have an economy rather than simply a culture in the older sense, but something has been given up. Similarly, if I delegate the censure of my neighbor to the police, I am less likely to search for nonpunitive alternatives than if I act simply as a neighbor. In a large group a police force is no doubt needed and we shall continue to have punitive governments, but the chances of working out better personal relations are then reduced.

When we delegate the control of people to political and economic institutions, we relinquish the face-to-face control of an equitable government of people by people, and it is a mistake to suppose that we recapture it by restricting the scope of those to whom we delegate it. *A better strategy is to strengthen face-to-face control.* A social environment, or culture, can operate without the help of usurping or delegated rulers and entrepreneurs, and it is most clearly a government of people by people when it does so. Something of the sort has been proposed from time to time—for example, in the political philosophy of anarchy—but nothing could better illustrate the failure to find appropriate means than the public stereotype of the anarchist as a man with a bomb. We are in a much better position today. We have begun to understand how the environment, particularly the social environment, works, and we already have some glimpses of how it can be made to work better.

Much of this has come about through the application of the experimental analysis of behavior, or what has come to be called behavior modification. One cannot use that term today without adding a caveat and a definition. I do not mean the modification of behavior by implanted electrodes or psychotropic drugs. I do not mean Pavlovian conditioning with vomit-inducing drugs or electric shock. By "behavior modification" I mean what the term was introduced to mean—changing behavior through positive reinforcement. The underlying processes have long been known and occasionally used, but we now have a better understanding of their role in the social environment and can therefore make significant changes in the face-to-face control of people by people.

Many people have had frightening visions of behavior modification in the hands of powerful governments or rich corporations, but the fact is that the major applications to date have been precisely at the level of the face-to-face control of people by people —by teachers who find better ways of working with students in the classroom and who use instructional materials which enable students to progress as rapidly as possible and with a minimum of aversive pressure, by attendants in hospitals and homes for psychotics and retardates who arrange conditions under which those in their care lead more interesting and dignified lives, by psychotherapists in face-to-face consultation with those who need help, by parents who discover how to make the family a warmer and more helpful institution, by employers who design incentive systems under which employees not only work well but enjoy what they do, and by individuals who discover how to manage their own lives effectively when face to face with themselves.

More than a hundred books have been published about behavior modification in the past five years and the rate of publication continues to rise. There is no indication that the principles are being sequestered or monopolized by individuals or organizations bent on exploitative control. On the contrary, the basic practices are finding their way into daily life as part of our culture. It is difficult to prescribe practices appropriate to a given situation. There are no general rules which will permit us to gloss over details. But some of the principles commonly observed in the application of an experimental analysis to daily life are worth noting because they are particularly concerned with the government of people by people. In one form or another they have a long history.

The very substitution of positive reinforcement for aversive control is, of course, at the heart of the struggle for freedom. Although we still have a long way to go, we have moved from slavery to the payment of wages, from the birch rod to the free school, and from bedlam to humane care of the psychotic and retarded. Positive reinforcement has a strengthening effect not only upon the behavior of the individual, but also upon the culture, by creating a world from which people are not likely to defect and which they are likely to defend, promote, and improve. All those who act to make the physical world more beautiful—the ecologists concerned with natural beauty and the artists, musicians, architects, and others who create beautiful things—all increase the chances that living in the world will be positively reinforced. Those who use behavior modification, properly defined, could be said to be concerned with preserving and furthering the beauty of the *social* environment—or, to borrow a phrase from a vanishing culture, to create more beautiful people.

A second principle in improving the control of people by people is *the avoidance of contrived reinforcers*. Here, again, there is a long history. We all live in a token economy. Money was invented as a conditioned reinforcer because it has many advantages: it is easily given and received; consuming the uncontrived reinforcers for which it is exchanged can be conveniently postponed; reinforcing values can be easily compared, and so on. But behavior is most expeditiously shaped and maintained by its natural consequences. The behavior of the production line worker which has no important consequence except a weekly wage suffers in comparison with the behavior of the craftsman which is reinforced by the things produced. The separation of workers from the natural products of their work was, of course, what Marx meant by "alienation." There is a similar effect when punitive sanctions are delegated to authorities, because negative reinforcers like fines or imprisonment alienate citizens from the direct censure of their peers.

There is nothing wrong with contrived reinforcers as such. Teachers and counselors need them to shape and strengthen behavior which the individual will find helpful in the natural contingencies in daily life. But contrived reinforcers must be abandoned before the preparation is complete. The student who continues to turn to a teacher has not been successfully taught; the client who continues to consult a counselor has not been successfuly counseled. The uncontrived reinforcers of the world at large must take over. The practices of industry and government are different. Workers must continue to receive the contrived reinforcers called wages, and citizens to be threatened with the contrived consequences called punishment. Alienation is then likely to follow.

A third principle is rather similar. *Behavior which consists of following rules is inferior to behavior shaped by the contingencies described by the rules.* Thus, we may learn to operate a piece of equipment by following instructions, but we operate it skillfully only when our behavior has been shaped by its effect on the equipment. The instructions are soon forgotten. Similarly, by learning the rules of a culture we are enabled to deal with people effectively, but our behavior will be most sensitive to the contingencies maintained "by the people" when we are directly censured and commended, and the rules of the culture, like the operating instructions for a piece of equipment, forgotten. (A familiar observation in jurisprudence is that laws survive long after the personal relationships they describe have changed, and they then misrepresent the prevailing social control.)

A fourth principle is not so widely recognized. *Control of people by people is likely to be disturbed by "noncontingent" reinforcers.* Many good things come to us free—from a bountiful climate, from a run of good luck, from other people who give them to us or allow us to take them without a struggle, or from a store of goods we have already accumulated. We count ourselves lucky when these potential reinforcers come our way when we have done nothing for them, but we should not overlook the damage they may do. Noncontingent reinforcers are characteristic of both affluence and welfare and have the same troublesome effects in both. By reducing the level of deprivation, they preempt many possibilities of reinforcement, and reinforcers of a lesser biological significance take over. The results are sometimes productive. We may turn to art, music, literature, science, or the other great achievements of the human species. More often, however, they are stultifying and wasteful—as when we turn to alcohol or other drugs, surrender to the variable-ratio schedules exploited by gambling systems, vicariously live the serious lives of others in gossip, literature, films, and spectator sports, or turn to violence as an escape from boredom. A policy of "work not welfare" may solve the problem of the noncontingent reinforcer for the unemployed, but not for the affluent. Noncontingent reinforcers keep the group from most fully developing the capacities of its members and threaten the strength of the culture and presumably its chances of survival.

Still another principle concerns the extent to which a culture prepares its members to meet its contingencies. A social environment is extraordinarily complex, and new members of a group do not come prepared with appropriate behavior. The individual was once inducted into a culture by natural instructional programs, in the presence of favorable models. These are no longer an important part of growing up, and more explicit control is now needed. Programmed sequences of contingencies, in the hands of skillful teachers and counselors, can lead efficiently to the complex repertoires demanded by a social environment.

These, then, are some of the principles to be observed in promoting the effective control of people by people. James Reston, writing in the *New York Times*, quoted the London *Economist* on the contribution America can make in its third century. It will depend, the *Economist* said, on how its three main institutions evolve. "These three main institutions are, in reverse order of importance, its business corporations, its government, and its mechanisms for living together"—in other words, the economy, the polity, and the culture in the older sense. Perhaps we may leave business to the economists and government to the political scientists, but to whom shall we assign the "mechanisms for living together," which the *Economist* puts at the top of the list? I submit that they are simply the contingencies which define the social environment as a culture and therefore precisely the field of a technology of behavior.

"Mechanisms for living together" compose the whole field of social psychology, but that does not mean that we can look to all social psychologists for help. A pure structuralism makes very little difference, and developmentalism not much more. The measurement of feelings and attitudes and other states of mind is scarcely a spur to action. Psychologists in general are not distinguished by any great readiness to act. Not only do they hesitate to change the behavior of other people, many of them strongly oppose any effort to do so. This narrows the field when we are looking for those who will contribute to our third century by improving our mechanisms for living together.

The trouble is that any allusion to the control of human behavior evokes the challenge: who will control?—often with the implication that a technology of behavior will naturally fall into the hands of despots. Like all sources of power it could very well do so, especially if those who are not despots refuse to act. But the very threat of misuse is the best reason for looking as clearly as possible at how a science of behavior can work "for the people." Behavior modifiers who stop intervening when their work is finished are certainly not classic examples of despotic rulers. True, they may pose a different threat. They are perhaps no more likely to engage in despotic control than atomic physicists to conquer the world with nuclear weapons, but will they not lend their skills as consultants to potential despots? A Machiavelli who uses his insights to advise a prince is perhaps as dangerous as the prince. But behavior modification is primarily a way of making people more effective, not in ruling others, but in maintaining and improving the social environments in which they live.

It is often said that in the end the question is who will control the controllers (*Quis custodiet ipsos custodes?*), but the issue is not *Who* but *What*. People act to improve cultural practices when their social environments induce them to do so. Cultures which have this effect and which support the relevant sciences are more likely to solve their problems and survive. It is an evolving culture, then, which is most likely to control the controller.

Unfortunately, it does not have the same effect on everyone. Those who act to improve government of the people by the people for the people have been selected by special, possibly accidental, circumstances. Since they have been selected, they are an elite, but they are not the exploiting elite that has given the word such bad connotations. Their task is not to control people but to bring people under the control of more effective physical and social environments. They operate upon the environment, not upon people.

Physical and biological technologists work with one part of that environment, as they construct contingencies affecting human behavior; and they do not in any sense remain in control of the people whom their achievements affect. Teachers, therapists, and other behavioral technologists work with another part of the environment—as they construct the contingencies under which people control people. But they themselves do not continue to intervene. We see this in miniature in such a field as family counseling. The counselor changes certain practices—for example, by teaching the members of a family to commend each other rather than criticize or complain—but the project is not finished until the family works more efficiently as a system without further intervention by the counselor. No cultural practice designed through the application of an experimental analysis of behavior involves a behavior modifier who *remains* in control. Control rests with "the people."

There will no doubt continue to be governmental and economic agencies, organizations, and institutions, for they have their proper functions, but they should not be given an exclusive franchise. A social environment functions most successfully for the individual, the group, and the species if, so far as possible, people directly control people. The design of a social environment in which they do so is one of our most pressing needs. It is quite clearly a special challenge to psychology as a science of behavior.

2

Are We Free
to Have a Future?

It is often pointed out that I have specialized in the behavior of rats and pigeons, and it is usually implied that as a result my judgment about people has been warped, but at least sixty percent of what I have published has been about human behavior. I have discussed government, religion, psychotherapy, education, language, incentive systems, art, literature, and many other human things. And so, of course, have thousands of other people, but I do not believe I have offered my readers just more of the same, for that is where the other 40 percent comes in. In writing about human affairs I have always stressed the implications of an experimental analysis of behavior, an analysis which was, indeed, first carried out on lower species, but which was eventually extended to human subjects with comparable results. Even the work with other species was relevant to human affairs, because it revealed the extraordinary role played by the environment in the determination of behavior. One did not need to believe that men and women were just like rats and pigeons to begin to look more closely at the world in which they lived. It became clear that certain features of that world had a bearing on some long-standing problems. What follows is offered as an example.

Doomsday prophecies are now a commonplace of daily life. We are continually reminded that, for all its past triumphs, mankind may be headed straight for disaster. Unless something is done, and soon, there will be too many people in the world, and they will ever more rapidly exhaust its resources and pollute its air, land, and water, until in one last violent struggle for what is left, some madman will release a stockpile of nuclear missiles. There are optimists, of course, who contend that the human species, like some other species, will prove to have some built-in mechanism which limits population (a mechanism more acceptable than the famine, plague, and war which have served that purpose in the past), that new and nonpolluting sources of energy will be discovered, and that some kind of world government or possibly the deterrent effect of even more horrible weapons will put an end to war. But the trend is certainly ominous, and Cassandra, who always prophesies disaster, may again be right. If so, it will be for the last time. If she is right now, there will be no more prophecies of any kind.

One of the most ominous things about the future is how little is being done about it. The great majority of the people on the earth do not know that there is a problem, and of those who know very few take any relevant action. A major difficulty is that the future always seems to conflict with the present. It may be obvious to commuters that their private cars are polluting the air they breathe, but a private car is nevertheless much more convenient than public transportation. Energy may be in short supply, but it is pleasant to heat buildings in the winter and cool them in the summer so that roughly the same kind of clothing can be worn in both seasons. Inflation undermines the future which would otherwise be provided for by personal savings or social security, but higher wages for labor and higher prices for management are momentarily rewarding. Overpopulation may be a major threat, but people take pleasure in procreation and pride in children. Wars may be inevitable so long as wealth is unevenly distributed, but those who are lucky enough to have an undue share naturally defend it. Physical and biological technologies are probably powerful enough to solve these problems and guarantee a decent future, but they will do so only if they are put to use. The problem is human behavior. How can people be induced to take the future into account? That is a question to which, I think, an analysis of behavior is relevant.

What does it mean to say that a person "takes the future into account" or acts in a given way "because of" something that will happen in the future? Can anything have an effect before it occurs? Final causes were soon ruled out of physics and eventually out of biology, but must we suppose that there is some way in which they function in the field of human behavior?

The traditional answer is yes. Human beings, it is said, differ from physical objects or non-human living things because they can *think* about the future. They can *imagine* the consequences of their action. They can act because they predict the future and therefore *know* what is going to happen. They can be affected by the mere *idea* or *concept* of a future. This is a mentalistic explanation of human behavior, of course, and it has the weakness which has always been the hallmark of mentalism. Thoughts, images, knowledge, ideas, and concepts are no explanation at all until they have been explained in turn. How do people come to think, imagine, have ideas, or develop concepts about the future? What does knowing about the future mean? Questions of this sort bear directly on the practical problem. Is it any easier to get people to think about the future than to get them to act with respect to it? In fact, are not the measures we say we take to change minds the very measures we take to change behavior? Even for the mentalist the problem is to get people to act *as if* they were thinking about the future. All we can change are the circumstances in which people live, and we want to change them in such a way that people will behave differently. We are on safer and more promising ground if we stick to the behavior.

Some biological processes are relevant to the problem of final causes. Although no future ever has an effect on the present, there is a sense in which living things are affected by consequences. An "effect of the future" was first recognized in Darwin's principle of natural selection. A genetic change or mutation does not occur because of any relation to the survival of the species, but if the resulting trait promotes survival, as it does in a few cases, the mutation becomes a characteristic of the species. We say that it enables the species to adapt or adjust to an environment, and adaptation and adjustment, like survival, point toward a future. Moreover, characteristics selected by past events seem *designed* to have an effect on the future. (The environment must remain essentially unchanged with respect to the features which have played a part in selection. Only that future is "taken into account" which resembles the past.)

The term "purpose" shows the change in formulation required. Before Darwin the purpose of any feature of the human body—say, the hand—seemed to lie in the future. A baby was born with a hand designed to grasp objects in the world in which it was to live. The theory of natural selection moved the significance of grasping into the past. A person is born with a hand which will be effective in his environment because his ancestors had hands which were effective in theirs. Procreation is an exclusive characteristic of living things; and it is the transmission of traits from generation to generation which makes natural selection an apparently creative principle "taking the future into account."

The individual organism is also affected by consequences. The process evolved through natural selection, but it operates on a very different scale. It was foreshadowed by philosophies of hedonism and fairly explicitly stated in Thorndike's Law of Effect. It has been most clearly demonstrated in the experimental analysis of operant conditioning. If a given bit of behavior has a consequence of a special sort, it is more likely to occur again upon similar occasions. The behavior is said to be strengthened by its consequences, and consequences having this effect are called reinforcers. For example, a foraging pigeon brushes aside a leaf lying on the ground and in doing so uncovers a seed; if the seed is reinforcing, the pigeon is more likely to brush aside similar leaves in the future.

In spite of the difference in time scale, operant conditioning bears a striking resemblance to natural selection. It builds an adaptation or adjustment to the environment. It seems designed to have an effect. It makes possible a similar disposition of purpose, moving it from the future into the past. All of this gives behavior a kind of orientation toward the future. (As in natural selection, the environment must be reasonably stable; behavior which is strengthened under a given set of circumstances will continue to be effective so long as the circumstances do not greatly change. The process "takes into account" a future which resembles the past.)

And only an immediate future. Operant conditioning would be maximally effective if it strengthened behavior which actually produced its consequences. Hedonism and the Law of Effect seemed to guarantee this because they both appealed to feelings—the pleasure and pain or satisfaction and annoyance which resulted from action. But the reinforcers which figure in the analysis of operant behavior are physical things, and they are consequences simply in the sense that they follow behavior. They need not be produced by it. The equipment used in the operant laboratory arranges temporal sequences only; there is no *functional* connection between a response and its effects. It is easy to show that a reinforcer which follows a response but has no other relation to it is effective; what we call superstition is an example.

This is a defect, and it must be attributed to the exigencies of natural selection. Operant conditioning evolved as a useful process in which behavior was brought under the control of *any* consequence, functional or not. It was useful because in general any event which followed an action was likely to have been produced by it. It was not necessary to take into account the reasons why a reinforcer occurred, and it is difficult to see how that could have been done.

The more immediate the consequence, the more likely it is to have been produced by the behavior it follows, but there are other reasons why reinforcement must be quick. If there is a delay, intervening behavior will be affected, possibly more strongly than the behavior responsible for the reinforcer. And reinforcement must *overlap* behavior if we are not to suppose that something which has not yet occurred can have an effect. The future mediated by operant conditioning is therefore not very remote.

(A possible exception was once called "stomach memory." In a laboratory demonstration, a rat is made sick a few hours after eating a particular kind of food and is then found to show a weakened preference for the food. If the rat is made sick through radiation, no intermediate activity can be involved. Such a mechanism should have great survival value in protecting organisms against indigestible or poisonous foods. The aversive consequence is anatomically linked to ingestion and "overlaps" it in that sense, and for the same reason it need not affect intervening behavior of other kinds. If the evidence is valid, a fairly remote future is mediated by this mechanism, but it is an exception. In general a reinforcer must be closely contingent on behavior if it is to be effective.)

Nevertheless, organisms do behave "because of" events which take place a long time in the future. A possible connection is made through a different process called respondent conditioning. The process probably evolved because it prepared organisms for unpredictable features of their environments. Foodstuffs like sugar and salt elicit salivation as an early step in digestion, but because sweet and salty foods vary greatly in appearance, organisms could not have developed the capacity to salivate appropriately to their mere appearances, no matter how important such a preparatory salivation might be. Through conditioning, the visual appearance of a particular food comes to elicit salivation, which is "directed toward the future"—though again not a very remote future.

Something of the sort affects the role of the stimulus in operant behavior. Sweet and salty foods reinforce the behavior of finding or capturing them, and they do so because organisms inclined to be so affected were more likely to survive and transmit the inclination. But, again, since foods vary widely in appearance, a susceptibility to reinforcement by the appearance of a food could have had little chance to evolve. What evolved instead was a process in which any occasion upon which behavior is likely to be reinforced becomes reinforcing in its own right.

Good examples appear when behavior is only intermittently reinforced. In a standard experiment a hungry pigeon must respond, say, 5000 times before a response is reinforced with a small amount of food. It must then respond 5000 times again before another response is reinforced. Shortly after reinforcement the pigeon could be said to be responding "because of" an event which lies in the fairly distant future. A ratio of 5000 to one can be maintained for hours, but only after a special program in which progress through the ratio *becomes* reinforcing.

Long chains of responses can be built up by conditioning reinforcers. In a typical classroom demonstration a rat executes a series of perhaps ten different responses, each of which is reinforced by the opportunity to execute the next, until a final, usually unconditioned, reinforcer appears. The first step seems to be taken "for the sake of the last," which lies in the fairly distant future. Something of the same sort occurs, when, for example, a person builds a shelter. The last step brings protection from the weather, but it can be taken only after earlier stages have been completed. As the shelter is constructed, each step is reinforced by the opportunity to take another step. (Not all sequences originate in this way, as we shall see, but once established they usually continue to be supported by some such arrangement of conditioned reinforcers.)

Even when supplemented by the conditioning of reinforcers, operant conditioning will not, without help, generate much of the human behavior which "takes the future into account." No individual could, in a single lifetime, acquire a very large repertoire in this way. A farmer plants in the spring "in order that he may harvest in the fall," but it is unlikely that anyone ever learned to do so for that reason alone. Another process comes into play. It involves other people, who accumulate and transmit useful behavior.

A basic process, imitation, may be part of the human genetic endowment. Other people have been a stable feature of the human environment, and a tendency to behave as others are observed to behave should have had great survival value; others presumably behave as they do for good reason, and by imitating them an individual can expediently acquire behavior useful for the same reason. Many species show innate imitative behavior, although its existence in man is still debated. In any case, there are contingencies of reinforcement, rather like those of survival, which induce people to behave as others are behaving. By imitating those whose behavior has already been shaped by prevailing contingencies, people acquire appropriate behavior without being directly exposed to the contingencies themselves. The customs and manners of a group seem to be maintained by such a process. With the help of imitation, individuals need not construct for themselves the long sequences which bring their behavior under the control of fairly remote consequences. They acquire much greater repertoires than would be possible in a nonsocial environment.

There are other arrangements of reinforcers which seem to bring the future more actively into play. Governmental practices supply good examples. The reinforcers used to "keep the peace" are almost exclusively aversive or punitive; for example, citizens are fined, flogged, or imprisoned when they behave illegally. The reinforcers used to induce citizens to defend a government against its enemies are also largely aversive; defectors and deserters are imprisoned or shot. A system of conditioned positive reinforcers is also used, ranging from medals to memorials. The behavior strengthened has consequences which reinforce the government for maintaining these conditions, but citizens may gain indirectly (if less immediately) from the order and security which result. Their behavior is due primarily to contrived governmental contingencies, but it has consequences in the possibly distant future which would be reinforcing if they occurred sooner. The governmental practice bridges a temporal gap.

Religious agencies also control their communicants with contrived reinforcers both positive and negative. The claimed power to determine extraordinary rewards and punishments after death is used first of all to strengthen the agency, but the communicant may acquire useful practices of self-control, as well as the advantages of living among well-behaved people.

Possibly the greatest of all conditioned reinforcers is money. Worthless in itself, it becomes reinforcing when exchanged for established reinforcers. Industry induces people to work by paying them. It enjoys relatively immediate gains, but people in general may profit from the resulting development and production of goods. Education shows the same pattern. The craftsman teaches his apprentice because he acquires a useful helper, but the apprentice gains by becoming a craftsman in his own right. It would be difficult to spot all the reasons why parents, peers, employers, religions, and governments contrive educational contingencies, but a distinction may still be drawn between the advantages gained by those who teach or pay for teaching and the possibly long-deferred gains of the learner. Ethical and moral practices are less conspicuously organized, but the same pattern prevails. People control each other—governing, teaching, giving incentives—because of immediate gains but in ways which yield possibly long-deferred advantages for all.

The consequences which lie in the possibly distant future are often cited to justify practices in government, religion, economics, education, and ethics. Governments may act primarily to maintain their power, but they seek legitimacy by pointing to peace and security. Religious agencies appeal to values such as peace of mind and compassion. Entrepreneurs justify themselves by pointing not to their profits but to the resources they develop and the goods they make available. And when a proposal is made to change a practice, it is usually supported by pointing to the deferred advantages rather than the immediate gains of those who propose it. Nevertheless, it is quite unlikely that the deferred consequences have any effect as reinforcers. They are, on the contrary, simply incidental by-products.

This is not to deny that they serve a different kind of function. The fact is that cultural practices have evolved in which contingencies of immediate reinforcement generate behavior having remote consequences, and this has presumably happened in part because the consequences have strengthened the culture, permitting it to solve its problems and hence survive. That the remote consequences, no matter how important for the culture, are nevertheless not having any current effect is all too evident when efforts are made to take into account a future which is not the by-product of currently reinforced behavior.

We have, of course, turned to various controlling agencies to forestall the disasters which threaten us. To reduce pollution, parts of cities are legally closed to private cars. Special lanes on bridges, in tunnels, and on highways are reserved for cars with a certain number of passengers or for buses. The use of energy is taxed. The manufacture of nondegradable detergents, herbicides, and insecticides is prohibited. Religious and legal sanctions against birth-control or abortion are eased, and economic incentives favoring large families are reduced or abolished. Children are taught to avoid waste, and campaigns in the mass media are designed to have the same effect on adults. We are to insist upon returnable bottles and cloth towels; we are to use recyclable handkerchiefs rather than tissues.

These measures are obviously taken for the sake of possibly long deferred consequences, but it has proved to be difficult to support them with immediate reinforcers. In fact, in democratic countries few if any institutional sanctions and suasions, designed for whatever purposes, are now working well. In our own culture, for example, people do not seem to be as law-abiding as they once were or as readily disposed to serve in the armed services. This does not mean that they have developed criminal tendencies or lost their patriotism; it means that laws are no longer as strictly enforced or military service as highly honored. We impose light punishments or suspend sentences, and in many states the death penalty has been abolished. We no longer shoot deserters, or glorify our heroes. (Only the returning prisoner of war is met with a brass band playing "See, the conquering hero comes!")

Fewer people now go to church or observe religious practices. This does not mean that they are less devout; it means that, as the Pope recently put it, a veil of silence has been drawn over the Devil.

Few theologians of my acquaintance mention hellfire, and most of them speak of heaven with a certain embarrassment.

Few people now work very hard. This does not mean that they have grown lazy; it means that economic incentives are no longer very effective. In the nineteenth century, it was believed that a hungry labor force was needed if industry was to prosper, but wages are now exchanged for goods which are less acutely needed than food. Welfare, like affluence, makes money less reinforcing; medicare and social security have replaced the threat of the poor farm, and even the prospect of a crystal palace is failing to recruit executive eager beavers.

More and more young people drop out of school and college. This does not mean they have lost their curiosity, their love of learning, or their desire for an education; it means that educational contingencies are no longer very compelling.

People no longer observe many of the social graces. This does not mean that they have become rude or thoughtless; it means that they are no longer consistently commended or punished by their peers. It has often been remarked that we no longer complain. In fact, the only behavior likely to be punished by one's peers is the behavior of complaint itself.

I have suggested elsewhere that this failure of institutional and ethical control can be attributed to certain features of the struggle for freedom. Men and women (exhibiting certain standard features of human behavior) escape from dangerous, irritating, annoying, or uncomfortable things. Among such things we must list the aversive measures used for purposes of control by other people, organized or unorganized. A person may escape from them by breaking contact—through defection, for example, or apostasy, truancy, or vagrancy—or by weakening or destroying their controlling power—by riots, say, or strikes, boycotts, or revolt. People are said to govern themselves—electing their own rulers, making their own mystical contact with God, sharing in the decisions made by the companies they work for, and so on. It is not surprising that they should not use strong measures, that they should avoid severe punishment and the extreme deprivation needed to make a small reward effective. They may end by destroying all forms of control, trusting to the human genetic endowment to survive without help.

The process can be followed in miniature in education. Instruction was once quite aversive. The Egyptians, the Greeks, and the Romans all beat their schoolboys, and medieval sculpture portrayed the schoolmaster with the tool of his trade, the birch rod. Corporal punishment is still with us. Positive reinforcers in the form of good marks, grades, promotion, diplomas, and prizes have been suggested but only as parts of ineffective contingencies of reinforcement. Rousseau proposed to solve the problem by letting students study what is naturally reinforcing. This is the strategy of the contemporary "free school." As a final step it has been suggested that schools be abolished, that the whole world be converted into a "learning environment."

Those who have proposed and effected changes of this kind have moved to destroy certain aversive or exploitative features of the environment. As a result people have more often felt free, and they have also probably enjoyed a greater sense of achievement or worth. But we can scarcely overlook the fact that some of the contrived contingencies under which human behavior has had important deferred consequences have been destroyed. As a result people are more susceptible to immediate consequences. It would be unfair to take the hippy culture as typical of American life today, but it served to point up certain features. Young people turned in large numbers to the immediate gratifications of drugs and sex, to forms of art and music which can be enjoyed without preparation, and to idleness as an escape from social and economic responsibilities. In doing so they had the support, often merely implicit, of several current philosophies—of existentialism with its rejection of both past and future, of phenomenology with its concentration on the experience of the moment, and of the structuralism of anthropology and linguistics with its neglect of causal factors lying outside the topography of behavior itself. They turned to mystical practices of the East, surrendering themselves, as one exponent has put it, "to the awareness of the present moment while forgetting the past and ignoring the future." Humanistic psychology added its support by emphasizing self-actualization, the meaning of which is perhaps clearer in French where *actuel* means current or contemporary.

Those who are alarmed by this excessive concern for immediate gratification are likely to argue that we should restore strong measures. All Communist countries and police states have taken this step, and stronger sanctions are being proposed in America. We are urged to make penalties more severe, restoring the death penalty for certain crimes including the sale of hard drugs, and enforce the law. The money people receive should be made more sensitively contingent on what they do. Welfare payments should depend on useful work. But this is not necessarily a way to make the future more effective. Stronger measures are also likely to be proposed for the sake of immediate consequences—for others. Powerful controllers are also committed to quick effects, and the remoter gains which sometimes occur as a kind of by-product are by no means guaranteed. The pendulum has swung from despotism through democracy to anarchy and back again many times, with little or no change in the future prospects of mankind. A stable equilibrium between control and countercontrol may occur from time to time, but equilibrium will not suffice.

We see the limitation of control and countercontrol in the incentive conditions in most industries. A hundred years ago the editor of the *Scientific American* wrote this: "We must fairly and honestly examine the conditions of the laboring classes, upon whom the whole structure of the social organism rests. The questions raised by them and in their behalf can never be adjusted by the two extremes—those anxious to secure the greatest possible amount of pay for the least possible work, and those anxious to obtain the greatest possible amount of work for the least possible pay." The opposing contingencies in industry are fairly obvious: employers control their employees with reinforcement, mostly monetary; the employees control employers with such measures as slowdowns, strikes, or boycotts. In what is called bargaining, conditions are worked out which are acceptable to both parties. The trouble is, they are not good conditions. They do not induce many people to work hard or carefully or enjoy what they are doing. Nor do they take into account the consequences for society as a whole, such as the usefulness of the product, the overall level of employment, or the development and conservation of resources.

The same limitations of control and countercontrol are seen in the other fields we have been examining. In government, for example, a system of checks and balances may make for a kind of stability but not for the most productive order; and between one government and another what is significantly called a balance of power yields at best the uneasy equilibrium we call peace.

We cannot continue to leave the future to the occasionally beneficial side effects of a strong concern for the present. Something more explicit must be done. But who will do it and why? Who are to plan for the future and under what conditions are they likely to do so? One possibility is that people will be more concerned for the future (for whatever reason) if they are less concerned for the present. Leaders in government, religion, and industry have sometimes thought about the future and acted with respect to it but they have usually done so only when their present problems appear to be solved. It is the successful government or governor who can afford to become benevolent. Very rich men have stopped using money to make more money and, especially when about to die, have set up foundations which are relatively free of present concerns and can act with respect to the future.

Other candidates for the custodianship of the future are to be found among those who have little or no power and hence little or nothing to gain from the present. In the nineteenth century, the press emerged as a "fourth estate." The government, the church, and the merchants represented the powers exerted through the police and military, the mediation of supernatural sanctions, and money, respectively. The press controlled no comparable reinforcers; it was limited to uncovering and reporting facts and exhorting to action, and it enjoyed little or nothing by way of immediate gain. The press was, therefore, concerned with the future, and it criticized the other three estates accordingly. From time to time it has been important enough to be suppressed by the other estates. A press which becomes the instrument of government, religion, or economic system can, however, no longer play this role.

Teachers satisfy the same specifications: They have little power, and teaching has few immediate consequences. The craftsman who teaches an apprentice quickly gains the advantage of having a useful helper, but teachers in schools, colleges, and universities are affected, if at all, by long-deferred results. Education is, indeed, primarily a preparation for the future; it gives the student current reasons for learning to behave in ways which will be useful later. Like the press, education serves this function only to the extent that it is not controlled by the current interests of a government, religion, or economic system.

We should expect that those most likely to take the future

into account will have two other qualifications which lie in the field of science. Whatever the reasons may be, people are more likely to act if they have a clear picture of the future. It does not take a scientist to be aware of changes in population, pollution, dwindling supplies of energy, and so on or to make rough extrapolations to the future, but science can do all this more effectively. It can collect data far beyond the range of personal experience, and it can project trends. The projections of the Club of Rome reported in *Limits to Growth* are an example.

Scientists should also be best able to say what can be done. The physical and biological sciences are needed if we are to redesign our cities to avoid the effects of crowding, to develop new forms of transportation, and to discover new sources of energy and new methods of contraception. Unfortunately physical and biological technology alone cannot guarantee that its solutions will be put into effect. To solve the major problem we need an effective technology of behavior. We need, in short, a new field of specialization—the design of cultural practices.

Frazier, the protagonist of *Walden Two,* is a kind of archetype. He has all the qualifications of the designer of the future. He wields none of the power to be found in a police force, in the mediation of supernatural sanctions, or in money. He has no personal power; to make that clear I gave him what might be called negative charisma. Since his place in the history of Walden Two has been deliberately concealed, he gains nothing by way of acclaim as a founder. He enjoys no special share of the proceeds of the community. He is, in short, the complete nonhero. In him the present has been almost totally suppressed; the future and its surrogates have taken complete control.

The specifications of that future were listed in *Beyond Freedom and Dignity.* Frazier has tried to construct a world in which "people live together without quarreling, maintain themselves by producing the food, shelter, and clothing they need, enjoy themselves and contribute to the enjoyment of others in art, music, literature, and games, consume only a reasonable part of the resources of the world and add as little as possible to its pollution, bear no more children than can be decently raised, continue to explore the world around them and discover better ways of dealing with it, and come to know themselves accurately and, therefore, manage themselves effectively." He has done this by constructing a social environment rich in immediate reinforcers, so selected that they strengthen the kinds of behavior which make a future possible.

And the reinforcers are positive. That is why the citizens of Walden Two feel free. Frazier himself, as the designer of a culture, is also under the control of positive consequences, no matter how remote. He has responded to the appeal of Utopian rather than Cassandran predictions—an important point. Threatening predictions sometimes spur action (it is perhaps just another sign of the weakness of the future that we so often respond only to threats), but they also induce people to escape simply by turning to other things. It is possible that we shall act more consistently with respect to the future when we see the possibility of building a better world rather than merely fending off disaster.

But something more is needed. Why should anyone design a better way of life? The answer has been waiting for us in the Utopian literature. An intentional commmunity emphasizes the issue of survival. The overriding question is: Will it work? It is not so obvious that the same question must be asked of every culture. It is asked, at least implicitly, by all those who are trying to solve the problems which face our culture today, and it must eventually be asked about mankind as a whole. Overpopulation, pollution, the exhaustion of resources, nuclear war—these are threats to the survival of the human race. Will the world that mankind has made for itself work?

And so we come at last to my title: Are we free to have a future? Put commas around "free" and the question is this: We who call ourselves free, are we to have a future? We call this the free world and America the land of the free. We insist that the wars we fight are fought in the defense of freedom. We value practices in government, religion, economics, education, and psychotherapy to the extent that they promote feelings of freedom. The question is whether practices *chosen for that reason* have survival value. Are they to make a major contribution to the future, or will practices chosen for different reasons by different people—say, the Chinese— displace them? The question once suggested a kind of social Darwinism, but cultural practices are no longer confined to any one territory, nation, race, religion, or economic system. What is evolving is a social environment, in which the genetic endowment of the human species will be maximally effective.

This is a test of freedom in the sense of a test of cultural practices selected because they make people feel free. We escape from or destroy aversive control when we can do so; that is the point of the struggle for freedom. When we act because we have been positively reinforced, we feel free and do not try to escape or countercontrol. The mistake is to believe that we are then actually free. This is not a philosophical or theological quibble. On the contrary, it is a point of the greatest practical importance.

Let us compare the lives of young people in China and the United States today. We say that young Americans are sexually free, while the Chinese, if we can trust the accounts, observe a strict moral code. We say that young Americans choose their work—or even not to work at all—while the Chinese are assigned to jobs and work long hours. Young Americans have access to a great variety of books, movies, theaters, and sports, but in China almost all of these are selected by the government. We say that young Americans choose where they are to live, while the Chinese have space assigned to them. Young Americans wear what they please; the Chinese wear standard uniforms. It is easy to exaggerate these differences. The Chinese no doubt have some choice, and not all Americans are free to choose their work or where they live. But, even so, the Americans seem to have much more freedom. Clearly, they have many more opportunities; they can do a great many more kinds of things. But are they really free to choose among them? Why, in fact, do they wear particular kinds of clothing, live in particular places, go to particular movies, work at particular jobs, or observe a particular sexual standard? Certainly the answer is not as easy as, "because the government tells them to do so," but that does not mean that there is *no* answer. It is much harder to demonstrate the control exerted by family, friends, education, religion, work, and so on, but it would be foolish to neglect it.

The *feeling* of freedom is another matter. It depends on the kinds of consequences responsible for behavior. Whether either Americans or Chinese feel free depends upon why they behave as they do. If young Chinese are conforming to their way of life because they will be denounced by their fellows and severely punished if they do not, we may be sure that they do not feel free. In that case they are doing what they have to do. But if Mao Tse-tung created a social environment rich in *positive* reinforcers, then they may be doing what they *want* to do, and it is quite possible that they feel freer than Americans. Moreover, it is possible that the reinforcers affecting their behavior have been chosen precisely because of their bearing on the future of the Chinese way of life.

Remove the commas, and my title is more to the point: Are we sufficiently free of the present to have a future? Our extraordinary commitment to immediate gratification has served the species well. The powerful reinforcing effects of drugs like alcohol and heroin are no doubt accidents, but our susceptibilities to reinforcement by food, sexual contact, and signs of aggressive damage have had great survival value. Without them the species would probably not be here today, but under current conditions they are almost as nonfunctional as drugs, leading not to survival but to obesity and waste, to overpopulation, and to war, respectively.

No matter how free we feel, we are never free of our genetic endowment or of the changes which occur in us during our lifetime. But if other aspects of human nature, aspects we sum up in the word intelligence, come into play, we may design a world in which our susceptibilities to reinforcement will be less troublesome and in which we shall be more likely to behave in ways which promise a future. The task can scarcely be overestimated. Happiness is a dangerous value, and the pursuit of happiness has clearly been too successful. Like other affluent nations, we must, to coin a horrid word, "deaffluentize." People have done so in the past when pestilence and famine have deprived them of natural reinforcers, and when revolutions in government and religion have changed their social environments, but the power of immediate reinforcement continues to reassert itself and with ever more threatening consequences. This could happen once too often. It is possible that the human species will be "consumed by that which it was nourished by." We have it in our power to avoid such an ironic fate. The question is whether our culture will induce us to do so.

3

The Ethics
of Helping People

We sometimes act for the good of others. We feed the hungry, clothe the naked, and heal the sick. We say that we care for them, provide for their needs, do good to them, help them. Our behavior often has unforeseen consequences which need to be taken into account.

We presumably help people in part for reasons that concern the survival of the species. Maternal behavior is a kind of help which is either part of an organism's genetic equipment or which is quickly acquired because of a genetic susceptibility to reinforcement; it is obviously important for survival. The human species is, presumably, more likely to survive if people generally help each other or are naturally reinforced by signs that they have done so. Something of the sort may contribute to the behavioral disposition which is part of what we call love or compassion.

It is more obvious that we learn to help or do good and that we learn because of the consequences which follow. We sometimes help because we find the helplessness of others aversive. We help those who help us in return, and we stop doing so when they stop —when, as we say, they are ungrateful. We often fail to help those who are too weak to reciprocate, or to protest effectively when we fail to help. The very young, the aged, the infirm, the retarded, and the psychotic are classic examples of people who often have been not only not helped but positively mistreated.

We may also help others because in doing so we further the survival of the group to which we belong. A social environment (a "culture") may induce us to give help even though we gain nothing directly from the advantage for the group. Thus, we may be a Good Samaritan at some personal sacrifice, and the group supplies overriding reasons for doing so with practices which have been selected simply because they have contributed to its survival. The group plays such a role when it steps in to guarantee adequate care for the very young, the aged, the infirm, the retarded, and the psychotic. There are few, if any, behavioral processes which provide for such care in the absence of a disposing social environment, with the possible exception of such genetic considerations as the care of the very young.

The sanctions arranged by a group are often treated in a different way. They are "justified" as defending individual *rights,* as guaranteeing that people shall get what they deserve or what is fair or just. It was perhaps easiest to justify helping those who were most in need of help, but, in many cultures, people are now said to have the right not only to life, liberty, and the pursuit of happiness, but to a share in the common wealth. "To each according to his [or her] need" was St. Augustine's program before it was Karl Marx's, and it is still a program, rather than an achievement. But it suggests the extent to which groups are now engaged in the business of making sure that their members help each other. The program is not without problems of an ethical nature. In solving them, all the consequences of an act of help must be considered. The following discussion deals with certain possibly relevant behavioral processes.

To begin with a very simple example, we may not really help others by doing things for them. This is often the case when they are learning to do things for themselves. We watch a child tying a shoelace, grow jittery, and to escape from our jitteriness, we "help" the child tie the lace. In doing so, we destroy one chance to learn to tie shoelaces. Comenius made the point nearly 400 years ago when he said that "the more the teacher teaches, the less the student learns." The metaphor of "communication," or the transmission and receipt of information, is defective at just this point. We ask students to read a text and assume that they then know what they have read. Effective communication, however, must provide for the so-called acquisition of knowledge, meaning, or information. A traditional method has been to repeat what is said, as in a verbose text. However, new methods in which textual help is progressively withdrawn have emerged in the field of programmed instruction. The aim is to give as little help as possible when readers are saying things for themselves.

By giving too much help, we postpone the acquisition of effective behavior and perpetuate the need for help. The effect is crucial in the very profession of helping—in counseling and psychotherapy. Therapists, like teachers, must plan their withdrawal from the lives of their clients. One has most effectively helped others when one can stop helping them altogether.

More serious unanticipated effects of the good we do to others often arise because "goods" function as "reinforcers." It has long been known that behavior is affected by certain kinds of consequences. That is why rewards and punishments are such well-established social measures. The Utilitarians proposed to quantify consequences in terms of pleasure and pain, for social purposes. For example, the pleasure enjoyed as the reward of unethical or illegal behavior was to be offset by a corresponding amount of pain administered as punishment. Both rewards and punishments were regarded as compensation; and when they were fairly balanced, the ethical account was closed.

The formulation neglected certain contingent relations between behavior and its consequences which were recognized by the American psychologist, Edward L. Thorndike, in his *Law of Effect*. By "effects" he also meant feelings, but they were more than compensation; they strengthened the connection between behavior and the situation in which it occurred. The strengthening effect of reinforcement has been an important consideration in the experimental analysis of operant behavior. Extremely complex environments are constructed in which reinforcing consequences are contingent upon both behavior and the setting in which it occurs; and the effect upon the probability that a given instance of behavior will occur upon a given occasion is analyzed.

The fact that strength in the sense of probability of occurrence is an important property of behavior has come to be understood only very slowly. With respect to the present issue, an important point is that strength is not related in any simple way to quantity of reinforcers and, therefore, not in any simple way to the help we give or the good we do to others, as these are traditionally evaluated. We need to consider the possibility that strength of behavior is more important than the receipt or possession of goods.

Those who are in a position to help others by giving them things can use the things as contingent reinforcers. This is, of course, the point of behavior modification. The right to change the behavior of others in this way has been challenged on ethical grounds, as we shall see, and Carl Rogers has suggested that the help given by the therapist (and one could also say teacher or friend) should be made carefully *non*contingent on the behavior of the recipient. Unfortunately, reinforcers are always temporally contingent on some behavior, and they are effective, even though there is no causal connection. Adventitious reinforcements build superstitions. For example, whatever people are doing just before rain falls at the end of a drought, they are more likely to do again in another drought. And since the more conspicuous their behavior, the more effective the adventitious contingencies, a ritual such as a rain dance may emerge, and in turn a myth to explain it—for example, as the propitiation of a giver of rain. The grace of God was defined by St. Paul as noncontingent upon works—"for if by works, then grace is no longer grace," and Rogers is proposing essentially that therapeutic help should have this divine quality. But there are behavioral processes which cannot be denied, and offerings and sacrifices to the Giver of Help are an important problem for the therapist.

Unanticipated consequences which follow when we are said to give people help can be much more serious. In an environment in which such things as food, shelter, and safety are guaranteed as rights, these things are less likely to serve as reinforcers. The recipients of bountiful help are rather in the position of those who live in a benign climate or possess great wealth. They are not strongly deprived or aversively stimulated and, hence, not subject to certain kinds of reinforcement. Some important forms of behavior are never acquired or, if they have been acquired, are no longer exhibited. But such people do not simply do nothing; instead, they come under the control of lesser reinforcers. No objection is likely to be raised to the classic examples found in art, music, literature, and scientific exploration. Individuals are encouraged to devote themselves to these fields through the kind of help called patronage or grants-in-aid. But these reinforcing consequences are, unfortunately, seldom as immediate or as personally effective as others, which have long given the leisure classes a special character. Sweets remain reinforcing to the nonhungry; alcohol and drugs have anomalous reinforcing effects; sexual reinforcement survives because we do not leave satiation to others; certain special schedules of reinforcement (such as those basic to all gambling devices) make weak reinforcers effective; and just the spectacle of other people living seriously or dangerously is often reinforcing, as in films or television.

These are the reinforcers, rather than those of art, music, literature, and science, which are more likely to be given free play by any help which preempts the serious business of life, and there is little to be said for them. Some are stultifying, and none leads to the full development of the human genetic potential. One's behavior may be reinforced for a lifetime in these ways and yet undergo almost no important change, and when these alternative reinforcers lose their power or are suppressed by societal rules, behavior falls to a very low ebb. We call the child who has been given excessive help "spoiled," and the term applies as well to the adult.

Organisms are at least as strongly disposed to take goods away from others as to supply them in the form of help, particularly when unmerited, and the disposition may serve as a natural corrective to excessive help. (We are inclined to speak of the feeling of compassion that accompanies helping others and the feeling of resentment that accompanies taking goods away from those who have not worked for them, but it is the tendencies to act which are involved here.) Aggressive behavior offsets or corrects compassionate help and may have survival value, for either species or group, if it leads to a more equitable distribution of goods, but *the question is not who should have how much of what but, rather, how they are to get what they have.*

The plight of those whose behavior is not often reinforced—because others do things for them, or because they have not learned to do things for themselves, or because they are given the things their behavior would otherwise be reinforced by—is familiar enough. Traditionally, their behavior is attributed to feelings and states of mind. Such people are said to lack initiative, to show little strength of character, to have weak wills, to lack spiritual strength, or to have egos that are not well developed. They are said to suffer from abulia (lack of will), acedia (spiritual torpor), apathy (lack of feeling), or boredom. *What they are suffering from is a world in which their behavior is not positively reinforced.*

It is easy to dismiss that statement as the idée fixe of a behavioral analyst, but strength of behavior, in the sense of the probability that behavior will occur, is a basic aspect of human nature. It is to be attributed to external contingencies of reinforcement, rather than internal deficiencies. Hence, it is an aspect about which something can be done. Something *is* being done by those who understand the importance of contingencies of reinforcement.

A good example of the neglect of relevant aspects of the environment is to be found in analyses of incentive conditions in modern industry.[1] The "degradation of labor" is said to have begun with the systematic destruction of craft skills. Workers move from craft to industrial conditions for many reasons. Work is usually easier and, because a task is divided among many workers, each share is simpler and can be learned during a briefer apprenticeship. Workers produce more in less time and can be paid more.

[1] Heilbroner, R. Review of Braverman, *Labor and Monopoly Capital: The Degradation of Work in the Twentieth Century. New York Review of Books,* Jan. 23, 1975.

Yet something has been lost. Many interpretations have appealed to feelings and states of mind: The worker has come to think of himself as a cog in a machine; he is no longer the possessor of the "accumulated knowledge of the materials and processes by which production is accomplished"; work has been reduced to "a series of bodily movements entirely devoid of meaning"; the worker is separated ("alienated") from the product of his labor; and so on. But why is this degrading? It is true that work on a production line is probably faster than the work of a craftsman without a deadline. Because it has been reduced in scope, it is also necessarily more repetitive and, hence, likely to yield the "fatigue of repeatedly doing the same thing" (not to be confused with physical exhaustion). Yet the gambler "works" fast and repetitiously and calls his life exciting; and the craftsman uses machines to save labor when he can and often works with a time-and-motion efficiency that an industrial engineer would give much to duplicate.

The important difference lies in the contingencies of reinforcement. It is often supposed that industrial workers work to get a reward, rather than avoid punishment. But as Marx and others have noted, they work because to do anything else would be to lose a standard of living maintained by their wages. They work under the eye of a supervisor upon whose report their continued employment depends. They differ from slaves only in the nature of the "punishment" they receive for not working. They are subject to *negative* reinforcement, a condition obscured by the uncritical use of the term reward.

The craftsman's behavior, in contrast, is reinforced at every stage by those conditioned reinforcers called signs of progress. A particular task may take a day, a week, a month, or a year, but almost every act produces something which will form part of the whole and is, therefore, *positively* reinforcing. It is this condition of "nondegrading" work which has been destroyed by industrialization, and some of those concerned with incentive conditions have used the principles of behavior modification to restore it.

A similar correction needs to be made to offset the unwanted by-products of helping others by supplying goods. Unfortunately, it is difficult to see this and to act accordingly just because our behavior in helping others is determined to such a large extent by reciprocal reinforcement. Given a choice between receiving something gratis and the opportunity to work to get it, those whom we help are likely to choose the former, and they will therefore more abundantly reinforce our behavior when we give them things rather than the opportunity to work for things. It is in the long run that the advantage of getting, rather than possessing, makes itself felt, both by them and by us, and what happens in the long run does not often have much of an effect. What a person is said to deserve as a right is subject to a similar bias.

It is just at this point that behavior modification plays a unique role. The term needs careful definition. Behavior has been modified ever since it was modifiable—which is to say, from the beginning. Behavior is modified by the threat of the bully or of the nation with a nuclear stockpile, by incentive tax allowances, by advertising, by religious rituals, by state lotteries and other gambling enterprises, and, recently, by certain physiological measures and explicit Pavlovian conditioning. The term was introduced, however, to refer to certain applications of the experimental analysis of behavior, particularly through the arrangement of contingencies of positive reinforcement. Behavior modification in that sense helps people by arranging conditions under which they *get* things rather than by *giving* them things. That is its essential feature. And for that very reason, it was inevitable that there would be some conflict with traditional views of helping others—especially with principles of what was just or fair or to be defended as the rights of the individual.

The issue first arose when behavior modification was used in institutional care. In many cultures, food, shelter, clothing, security, and possibly privacy have been made available to those who for any reason cannot otherwise obtain them. Homes for the very young, the aged, the infirm, and the retarded, hospitals for psychotics, and prisons are far from a benign world, but those who live in them, characteristically, have little reason to work for the basic reinforcers because the reinforcers have been guaranteed as rights. Most of the alternatives, such as gambling, sex, alcohol, and drugs, are not available (except surreptitiously in prisons). As a result, such people suffer all the ills of having nothing to do.

Troublemaking may be unintentionally reinforced, and if possible they escape, but otherwise we say that their behavior tends to be marked by boredom, abulia, acedia, and apathy.

Behavior modification, properly defined as "the applied analysis of behavior," is precisely what is needed to correct this shortcoming of institutional life *because it is concerned with establishing effective contingencies of reinforcement.* Actual practices need not be described here, but the behavior modifier usually begins with a search for available reinforcers and then arranges especially clear-cut contingencies—as with the use of tokens. Contingencies can be programmed to shape complex topographies and to bring behavior under the control of complex stimuli. For those who will eventually leave the institution, such a program is called educational, therapeutic, or rehabilitative. For those who must remain, the goal is simply a "prosthetic" environment—an environment in which people behave in reasonably effective ways in spite of deficiencies, in which they take an active interest in life and begin to do for themselves what the institution previously did for them.

Whether we are concerned with education, therapy, and rehabilitation, or with the construction of a prosthetic environment, we need those reinforcers which have acquired special power in the evolution of the species. Yet they are the very things supplied in the act of helping or caring for people—the things guaranteed as rights. In order to make them contingent on behavior in an institutional setting, we must withhold them until the behavior occurs. The individual must, therefore, be deprived to some extent and, consequently, will appear to remain unhelped or to be denied certain rights. We cannot avoid this conflict so long as we continue to view help as providing goods rather than as arranging contingencies of reinforcement.

The conflict first came into the open in an attack upon operant reinforcement programs in mental hospitals. One set of proposed regulations contained the following:

> "Deprivation is never to be used. No patient is to be deprived of expected goods and services and ordinary rights, including the free movement of his limbs, that he had before the program started. In addition deficit rewarding must be avoided; that is, rewards must not consist of the restoration of objects or privileges that were taken away from the patient or that he should have had

to begin with. The ban against deficit rewarding includes
the use of tokens to gain or regain such objects or privi-
leges." [2]

The authors insist that they are concerned with the legitimacy
of the rationale for using operant conditioning, but it is the rationale
of rights which is at issue. Why have these things been guaranteed
to the patient? What "should" patients have had to begin with?
The mistake is to generalize from those who cannot help themselves
to those who can. For the latter, a much more fundamental right—
the right to live in a reinforcing environment—must be considered.
If the function of an institution is education, therapy, or rehabilitation, all available resources should be used to speed the process, and
the strong reinforcers are undoubtedly to be classified as such. For
those who will never return to the world at large, a strongly reinforcing environment is equally important.

Under proper contingencies, many institutionalized people
can engage in productive work, such as caring for themselves, keeping their quarters clean, and working in laundry, kitchen, or truck
garden. But when these things have previously been done by paid
personnel, suspicion falls on the motives of management. Should
residents not be paid the same wages? One answer is that they
should unless the contingencies are "therapeutic," but that raises
the question of help in only a slightly different form. Residents
are receiving help when their behavior is being reinforced in a
prosthetic environment, though they are not necessarily being
"cured." Especially when we consider the economics of institutional
care, can there be any objection to the residents themselves producing all the goods and services it was once supposed to be
necessary for others to give them?

At least one state has recognized the issue. A bill was recently
passed in Iowa with the provision that:

"The administrator may require of any resident of the
County Care Facility with the approval of a physician
reasonable and moderate labor suited to the resident's

[2] Lucero, R. J., Vail, D. J., and Scherber, J. Regulating operant–
conditioning programs. *Hospital and Community Psychiatry*, 1968,
19(2), 53–54.

age and bodily strength. Any income realized through the labor of a resident together with the receipts from operation of the County Farm if one is maintained shall be appropriate for use by the County Care Facility in such manner as the Board of Supervisors may direct." [3]

The constitutionality of the bill is being questioned.

The so-called rehabilitation of the prisoner raises a special problem. Prisoners usually undergo very little useful change. They have been separated from society for the latter's protection or as punishment and are unable to help themselves only because they have been cut off from the usual means. The destructive changes which follow are well known. Some promising results have been obtained from the application of an experimental analysis of behavior—for example, in a project at the National Training School for Boys in Washington, D.C.[4] Unfortunately, experiments of this sort have been confused with efforts to change prisoners with drugs or the more violent forms of aversive conditioning, and protests against the latter—for example, by the American Civil Liberties Union—have been extended without warrant to efforts to construct more sustaining prison environments.

Like everything else, operant conditioning can be misused. Management may solve some of its problems by arranging contingencies which suppress disruptive behavior and under which a child, a prisoner, or a psychotic may simply sit quietly and do little or nothing all day long. Even so, this may be better than achieving the same result through punishment, but both solutions may be challenged if nothing further is done. Much more can be done through the applied analysis of behavior when the problem is understood.

Some of the same issues arise in the world at large, where helping people takes on a much broader meaning. Very little has

[3] *Behavioral Voice* § 5 (Center for Human Development, Drake University, Des Moines, Iowa). (The bill is called "The Redesignation of County Homes as County Care Facilities," HF659.)

[4] Cohen, H. L., and Filipczak, J. *A new learning environment.* San Francisco: Jossey-Bass, 1971.

ever been achieved simply by supplying goods and services. Governments do not help their citizens by *giving* them order and security —that is the claim only of the police state; they help them by arranging environments in which they behave in orderly and mutually supportive ways. They do not defend the rights to life, liberty, and the pursuit of happiness as things which their citizens *possess;* they maintain environments in which people do not threaten the lives and political freedom of one another. Schools and colleges do not *give* their students information, knowledge, or skills; they are environments in which students acquire informed and skillful behavior. The "good life" is not a world in which people *have* what they need; it is one in which the things they need figure as reinforcers in effective contingencies.

A case history will show how easily the basic issue is missed. After the Second World War, Denmark entered upon a program of "modern reformatory guidance" to raise the standard of living of the Eskimos of Greenland.[5] Thousands of construction workers were sent in to build modern houses and facilities. But the local industry, fishing, could not support these material standards, and an annual subsidy of many millions of dollars will now be needed —indefinitely—for the 50,000 inhabitants. The goods supplied are not contingent on productive behavior, and it is not surprising that a long-established, cooperative culture has broken down. Under the surface, there is said to be "an alarming chaos of human frustration." An antagonistic class society is developing. Good dyadic social relations have yielded to drunken brawls.

It means little to say that a high standard of living was "an artificial creation," that it can be made natural by giving each person a more direct influence in government, or that a "strategy of wholeness" is needed. The trouble is that certain basic contingencies of reinforcement have been destroyed. And it is difficult to see how they can ever be restored except by greatly increasing the behavioral repertoires of the Eskimos or by sharply reducing their so-called standard of living. It will not be enough that the teams of construction workers are now to be followed by teams of social workers. The United States is repeating the experiment on a small

[5] Jensen, B. Human reciprocity: An Arctic exemplification. *American Journal of Orthopsychiatry,* 1973, *43,* 447-458.

scale on the island of Bikini, and it will be interesting to see whether the result is the same.

Even in the restricted sense of the applied analysis of behavior, behavior modification has grown with astonishing speed and much of that growth has been uncharted and chaotic. Practitioners have ranged from scientists highly skilled in the basic analysis to laymen applying a few cookbook rules. But the accomplishments are too substantial to be dismissed—among them, programmed instruction and contingency management in the classroom, the design of prosthetic environments for the retardate and psychotic, personal and family counseling in ethical self-management, educational environments for juvenile delinquents, and new incentive systems in industry. In retrospect, much of this often seems to be simply a matter of common sense, but people have had common sense for thousands of years, and it has not helped them solve the basic problem. It has been too easy to put possession ahead of acquisition, and to miss the importance of strength of behavior and its relation to contingencies of reinforcement. In the classroom, hospital, factory, prison, home, and the world at large, the obvious fact is that some of the good things in life are in short supply. We are just beginning to see that a mere shortage is not what is causing trouble and that people will not necessarily be helped by increasing the supply. Behavior modification through the management of contingencies of reinforcement is a special way of helping people just because it is concerned with changing the probability that they will behave in given ways.

For just that reason, it is now under attack. A recent example is the report of the Ervin Committee, *Individual Rights and the Federal Role in Behavior Modification,* based on a three-year investigation of federal support of a variety of programs. According to Senator Ervin, "The most serious threat posed by the technology of behavior modification is the power this technology gives one man to impose his views and values on another. . . . If our society is to remain free, one man must not be empowered to change another man's personality." [6] But individuals have always had the

---

[6] "Individual Rights and the Federal Role in Behavior Modification," No. 5270–02620.

power to impose their views on others; the relevant behavioral processes were not recently invented. One of the greatest and certainly the most convenient of all reinforcers is money, and we have recently seen some extraordinary examples of its misuse. Why does the Ervin Committee not consider constitutional safeguards against the power which a person can amass by accumulating money? We have minimum wage laws and other laws restricting some uses of money, but we have no maximum wage laws restricting the extent to which money can be acquired for use. And money is only one of the more conspicuous instruments of control. Possibly, the experimental analysis of behavior will play its greatest role in forcing an examination of *all* the ways in which "one man can change another man's personality."

Like any other means of control—say, physical force—behavior modification should be supervised and restrained. The concept of the rights of the individual is concerned with that problem. Some traditional principles have emphasized freedom from coercive or punitive control, and they are as badly needed today as they have ever been. Other traditional principles have emphasized the possession of goods and services, and here a sweeping revision is needed. Neither a capitalist defense of private property nor a socialist program of state ownership as a means of equitable distribution takes into account the full scope of relevant behavioral processes.

It has been suggested that Gross National Product should be subordinated to Gross National Happiness in evaluating a culture, but nothing much would be gained if happiness were identified as a static condition of satisfaction derived from the possession of goods. Indeed, in that case, there would scarcely be a distinction. The greatest good of the greatest number may be the greatest bore, and the Utilitarians lost their case just because they neglected the reinforcing contingencies which build the condition we describe by saying that we are happy.

The intense current interest in ethical, moral, legal, and religious matters is no doubt largely a response to worsening world conditions. A burgeoning population forces us to take another look at birth control, abortion, and selective breeding. Increasing violence, as in bombings, hijackings, and political kidnappings, forces us to look again at legal sanctions, possibly reversing a humane trend against capital punishment. In addition, however, a surprising number of critical issues have to do with what is called helping people. "Aid" is a synonym of "help," and foreign aid raises many ethical, moral, and legal problems. In the name of aid, the United States has become one of the Zaharoffs of the last half of the twentieth century—one of the great munitions makers who were once held in utter contempt. In the name of aid, we rescue some of the starving peoples of the world while allowing others to die, and refuse to admit that we are practicing triage. With both military and nonmilitary "help," we have nearly destroyed Indochina. And so we begin again to ask to what extent the rich nations of the world are to help the poor, or, in domestic affairs, how far a government should go in increasing the help which its rich citizens must give to its poor? [7]

But it is a mistake to turn again to certain earlier principles. For reasons which in themselves illustrate a powerful behavioral principle, we have grossly overemphasized the importance of simple possession. Neither happiness nor the survival of the group depends on the satisfaction derived from having things. And the most generous help may fail as ignominiously as the most aggressive despoliation. Something else is needed to achieve conditions under which human beings will show the productivity, the creativity, and the strength inherent in their genetic endowment and which are essential to the survival of the species.

[7] Rawls, J. *A theory of justice.* Harvard University Press, 1971. Nozick, R. *Anarchy, state, and utopia.* Basic Books, 1974.

4

Humanism and Behaviorism

There seem to be two ways of knowing, or knowing about, another person. One is associated with existentialism, phenomenology, and structuralism. It is a matter of knowing what a person is, or what he is like, or what he is coming to be or becoming. We try to know another person in this sense as we know ourselves. We share his feelings through sympathy or empathy. Through intuition we discover his attitudes, intentions, and other states of mind. We communicate with him in the etymological sense of making ideas and feelings common to both of us. We do so more effectively if we have established good *interpersonal* relations. This is a passive, contemplative kind of knowing: If we want to predict what a person does or is likely to do, we assume that he, like us, will behave according to what he is; his behavior, like ours, will be an expression of his feelings, states of mind, intentions, attitudes, and so on.

The other way of knowing is a matter of what a person *does*. We can usually observe this as directly as any other phenomenon in the world; no special kind of knowing is needed. We explain why a person behaves as he does by turning to the environment rather than to inner states or activities. The environment was effective during the evolution of the species, and we call the result the human genetic endowment. A member of the species is exposed to another part of that environment during his lifetime, and from it he acquires a repertoire of behavior which converts an organism with a genetic endowment into a person. By analyzing these effects of the environment, we move toward the prediction and control of behavior.

But can this formulation of what a person *does* neglect any available information about what he *is?* There are gaps in time and space between behavior and the environmental events to which it is attributed, and it is natural to try to fill them with an account of the intervening state of the organism. We do this when we summarize a long evolutionary history by speaking of genetic endowment. Should we not do the same for a personal history? An omniscient physiologist should be able to tell us, for example, how a person is changed when a bit of his behavior is reinforced, and what he thus becomes should explain why he subsequently behaves in a different way. We argue in such a manner, for example, with respect to immunization. We begin with the fact that vaccination makes it less likely that a person will contract a disease at a later date. We say that he becomes immune, and we speak of a state of immunity, which we then proceed to examine. An omniscient physiologist should be able to do the same for comparable states in the field of behavior. He should also be able to change behavior by changing the organism directly rather than by changing the environment. Is the existentialist, phenomenologist, or structuralist not directing his attention precisely to such a mediating state?

A thoroughgoing dualist would say no, because for him what a person observes through introspection and what a physiologist observes with his special techniques are in different universes. But it is a reasonable view that what we feel when we have feelings are states of our own bodies, and that the states of mind we perceive through introspection are other varieties of the same kinds of things. Can we not, therefore, anticipate the appearance of an omniscient physiologist and explore the gap between environment and behavior by becoming more keenly aware of what we are?

It is at this point that a behavioristic analysis of self-knowledge becomes most important and, unfortunately, is most likely to be misunderstood. Each of us possesses a small part of the universe

within his own skin. It is not for that reason different from the rest
of the universe, but it is a private possession: We have ways of
knowing about it that are denied to others. It is a mistake, however,
to conclude that the intimacy we thus enjoy means a special kind
of understanding. We are, of course, stimulated directly by our own
bodies. The so-called interoceptive nervous system responds to conditions important in deprivation and emotion. The proprioceptive
system is involved in posture and movement, and without it we
could scarcely behave in a coordinated way. These two systems,
together with the exteroceptive nervous system, are essential to
effective behavior. But knowing is more than responding to stimuli.
A child responds to the colors of things before he "knows his colors."
Knowing requires special contingencies of reinforcement that must
be arranged by other people, and the contingencies involving private events are never very precise because other people are not
effectively in contact with them. In spite of the intimacy of our own
bodies, we know them less accurately than we know the world
around us. And there are, of course, other reasons why we know
the private world of others even less precisely.

The important issue, however, is not precision but subject
matter. Just what can be known when we "know ourselves"? The
three nervous systems just mentioned have evolved under practical
contingencies of survival, most of them nonsocial. (Social contingencies important for survival must have arisen in such fields as
sexual and maternal behavior.) They were presumably the only
systems available when people began to "know themselves" as the
result of answering questions about their behavior. In answering
such questions as "Do you see that?" or "Did you hear that?" or
"What is that?" a person learns to observe his own responses to
stimuli. In answering such questions as "Are you hungry?" or "Are
you afraid?" he learns to observe states of his body related to deprivation and emotional arousal. In answering such questions as
"Are you going to go?" or "Do you intend to go?" or "Do you feel
like going?" or "Are you inclined to go?" he learns to observe the
strength or probability of his behavior. The verbal community asks
such questions because the answers are important to it, and in a
sense it thus makes the answers important to the person himself.
The important fact is that such contingencies, social or nonsocial,
involve nothing more than stimuli or responses; *they do not involve*

mediating processes. We cannot fill the gap between behavior and the environment of which it is a function through introspection because, to put the matter in crude physiological terms, we do not have nerves going to the right places. We cannot observe the states and events to which an omniscient physiologist would have access. What we feel when we have feelings and what we observe through introspection are nothing more than a rather miscellaneous set of collateral products or by-products of the environmental conditions to which behavior is related. (We do not act because we feel like acting, for example; we act *and* feel like acting for a common reason to be sought in our environmental history.) Do I mean to say that Plato never discovered the mind? Or that Aquinas, Descartes, Locke, and Kant were preoccupied with incidental, often irrelevant by-products of human behavior? Or that the mental laws of physiological psychologists like Wundt, or the stream of consciousness of William James, or the mental apparatus of Sigmund Freud have no useful place in the understanding of human behavior? Yes, I do. And I put the matter strongly because, if we are to solve the problems that face us in the world today, this concern for mental life must no longer divert our attention from the environmental conditions of which human behavior is a function.

But why have we attached so much importance to our feelings and states of mind, to the neglect of the environment? The answer seems to lie in the immediacy and the saliency of the stimuli. Many relevant events in our personal history pass without notice. For one thing, the behavior to which they will eventually prove relevant has not yet occurred and cannot contribute to contingencies that would lead us to notice them. And if we have noticed them, we may quickly forget. But our feelings, "ideas," "felt intentions," and so on, often overlap the behavior to which they seem related, and they usually occur in just the place that would be occupied by a cause (on the principle of *post hoc, ergo propter hoc*). For example, we often feel a state of deprivation or emotion before we act in an appropriate way. If we say something to ourselves before saying it aloud, what we say aloud seems to be the expression of an inner thought. And if we say something aloud without first saying it to ourselves, it is tempting to suppose that we must be expressing a nonverbal thought.

This apparent causality lodged within the private world

within a skin, together with the organization imposed upon it by the fact that all its determining conditions have occurred in the history of one person, generates a "sense of self." We feel there is an "I" who knows what he is going to do and does it. Each of us is aware or conscious of at least one such self, which we learn to manage more or less effectively.

Since the only selves we know are human selves, it is often said that man is distinguished from other species precisely because he is aware of himself and participates in the determination of his future. What distinguishes the human species, however, is the development of a culture, a social environment that contains the contingencies generating self-knowledge and self-control. It is this environment that has been so long neglected by those who have been concerned with the inner determination of conduct. The neglect has meant that better practices for building self-knowledge and self-management have been missed.

It is often said that a behavioristic analysis "dehumanizes man." But it merely dispenses with a harmful explanatory fiction. In doing so it moves much more directly toward the goals that fiction was designed, erroneously, to serve. People understand themselves and manage themselves much more effectively when they understand the relevant contingencies.

Important processes in self-management lie in the fields of ethics and morals, where conflicts between immediate and deferred consequences are considered. One of the great achievements of a culture has been to bring remote consequences to bear upon the behavior of the individual. We may design a culture in which the same results will be achieved much more efficiently by shifting our attention from ethical problem solving or moral struggle to the external contingencies.

We may move from an inner agent to environmental determinants without neglecting the question of values. It has been argued that behaviorism is or pretends to be value free, but that no value-free science can properly deal with man *qua* man. What is wrong in the traditional argument can be seen in the expression "value judgment." An inner initiating agent is to *judge* things as good or bad. But a much more effective source of values is to be found in the environmental contingencies. The things people call good are positive reinforcers, and they reinforce because of the contingencies of survival under which the species has evolved. Until recently, the species could survive famine, pestilence, and other catastrophes only if its members procreated at every opportunity, and under such contingencies sexual contact became highly reinforcing. Sex is not reinforcing because it feels good; it is reinforcing *and* feels good for a common phylogenic reason. Some reinforcers may acquire their power during the life of the individual. Social goods, such as attention or approval, arc created and used to induce people to behave in ways that are reinforcing to those who use them. The result may be good for the individual as well as for others, particularly when deferred consequences are mediated.

The values affecting those who are in charge of other people supply good examples of the importance of turning from supposed attributes of an inner man to the contingencies affecting behavior. There are five classical types of human beings who have been mistreated: the young, the elderly, prisoners, psychotics, and retardates. Are they mistreated because those who are in charge of them lack sympathy, compassion, or benevolence, or have no conscience? No, the important fact is that they are unable to retaliate. It is easy to mistreat any one of these five kinds of people without being mistreated in turn. The confrontation in 1972 between Humanists and Catholics at the LaFarge Center in New York City failed to make clear that the *sources* of conscience are not to be found in psychological realities but in punitive sanctions.

An environmental analysis has a special advantage in promoting a kind of value concerned with the good of the culture. Cultures evolve under special contingencies of survival. A practice that makes a culture more likely to survive survives with the culture. Cultures become more successful in meeting contingencies of survival as they induce their members to behave in more and more subtle and complex ways. (Progress is not inevitable, of course, for there are extinct cultures as well as extinct species.) An important stage is reached when a culture induces some of its members to be concerned for its survival, because they may then design more effective practices.

Over the years, men and women have slowly and erratically constructed physical and social environments in which they have come closer to fulfilling or actualizing their potential. They have not changed themselves (that is a genetic problem which has not yet been solved); they have changed the world in which they live. In the design of his own culture, man could thus be said to control his destiny.

I would define a humanist as one of those who, because of the environment to which he has been exposed, is concerned for the future of mankind. A movement that calls itself "humanistic psychology" takes a rather different line. It has been described as "a third force" to distinguish it from behaviorism and psychoanalysis; but "third" should not be taken to mean advanced, nor should "force" suggest power. Since behaviorism and psychoanalysis both view human behavior as a determined system, humanistic psychologists have emphasized a contrast by defending the autonomy of the individual. They have insisted that a person can transcend his environment, that he is more than a causal stage between behavior and environment, that he determines what environmental forces will act upon him—in a word, that he has free choice. The position is most at home in existentialism, phenomenology, and structuralism, because the emphasis is on what a person is or is becoming. Maslow's expression "self-actualization" sums it up nicely: The individual is to fulfill himself—not merely through gratification, of course, but through "spiritual growth."

Humanistic psychologists are not unconcerned about the good of others or even the good of a culture or of mankind, but such a formulation is basically selfish. Its development can be traced in the struggle for political, religious, and economic freedom, where a despotic ruler could be overthrown only by convincing the individual that he was the source of the power used to control him. The strategy has had beneficial results, but it has led to an excessive aggrandizement of the individual, which may lead in turn either to new forms of tyranny or to chaos. The supposed right of the individual to acquire unlimited wealth which he is free to use as he pleases often results in a kind of despotism, and the Hindu concern for personal growth in spirituality has been accompanied by an almost total neglect of the social environment.

Better forms of government are not to be found in better rulers, better educational practices in better teachers, better economic systems in more enlightened management, or better therapy in more compassionate therapists. Neither are they to be found in better citizens, students, workers, or patients. The age-old mistake is to look for salvation in the character of autonomous men and women rather than in the social environments that have appeared in the evolution of cultures and that can now be explicitly designed.

By turning from man *qua* man to the external conditions of which man's behavior is a function, it has been possible to design better practices in the care of psychotics and retardates, in child care, in education (in both contingency management in the classroom and the design of instructional material), in incentive systems in industry, and in penal institutions. In these and many other areas we can now more effectively work for the good of the individual, for the greatest good of the greatest number, and for the good of the culture or of mankind as a whole. These are certainly humanistic concerns, and no one who calls himself a humanist can afford to neglect them. Men and women have never faced a greater threat to the future of their species. There is much to be done and done quickly, and nothing less than the active prosecution of a science of behavior will suffice.

5

Walden Two Revisited

The early summer of 1945, when I wrote *Walden Two,* was not a bad time for Western Civilization. Hitler was dead, and one of the most barbaric regimes in history was coming to an end. The Depression of the thirties had been forgotten. Communism was no longer a threat, for Russia was a trusted ally. It would be another month or two before Hiroshima would be the testing ground for a horrible new weapon. A few cities had a touch of smog but no one worried about the environment as a whole. There were wartime shortages, but industry would soon turn again to devoting unlimited resources to the fulfillment of unlimited desires. The industrial revolution was said to have stilled the voice of Thomas Robert Malthus.

The dissatisfactions which led me to write *Walden Two* were personal. I had seen my wife and her friends struggling to save themselves from domesticity, wincing as they printed "housewife" in those blanks asking for occupation. Our older daughter had just finished first grade, and there is nothing like a first child's first year in school to turn one's thoughts to education. We were soon to leave Minnesota and move to Indiana and I had been in search of housing. I would be leaving a group of talented young string players who had put up with my inadequacies at the piano and I was not sure I could ever replace them. I had just finished a productive year on a Guggenheim Fellowship, but I had accepted the chairmanship of a department at Indiana and was not sure when I would again have time for science or scholarship. Was there not something to be done about problems of that sort? Was there not by any chance something a science of behavior could do?

It was probably a good thing that these were small provincial problems, because I might not have had the courage to tackle bigger ones. In *Behavior of Organisms,* published seven years earlier, I had refused to apply my results outside the laboratory. "Let him extrapolate who will," I had said. But, of course, I had speculated about the technology that a science of behavior implied and about the differences it could make. I had recently been taking the implications seriously because I had been meeting once a month with a group of philosophers and critics (among them Herbert Feigl, Alburey Castell, and Robert Penn Warren) where the control of human behavior had emerged as a central topic.

That all this should come together in a novel about a utopian community was probably due to the fact that a colleague, Alice F. Tyler, had sent me a copy of her new book, *Freedom's Ferment,* a study of perfectionist movements in America in the nineteenth century.[1] With two months to spare before moving to Indiana, I decided to write an account of how I thought a group of, say, a thousand people might have solved the problems of their daily lives with the help of behavioral engineering.

Two publishers turned *Walden Two* down, and Macmillan published it only on condition that I write an introductory text for them. These editorial judgments were, at the time, quite correct. One or two distinguished critics took the book seriously, but the public left it alone for a dozen years. Then it began to sell, and the annual sales rose steadily on a compound interest curve.

There were, I think, two reasons for the awakened interest. The "behavioral engineering" I had so frequently mentioned in the book was, at the time, little more than science fiction. I had

[1] Tyler, A. F. *Freedom's Ferment.* Minneapolis: Univ. of Minnesota Press, 1944.

thought that an experimental analysis of behavior could be applied to practical problems, but I had not proved it. The 1950s, however, saw the beginnings of what the public has come to know as behavior modification. There were early experiments on psychotic and retarded persons, and then on teaching machines and programmed instruction, and some of the settings in which these experiments were conducted were in essence communities. And in the sixties applications to other fields, such as counseling and the design of incentive systems, came even closer to what I had described in *Walden Two*. A technology of behavior was no longer a figment of the imagination. Indeed, to many people it was altogether too real.

But there was, I think, a better reason why more and more people began to read the book. The world was beginning to face problems of an entirely new order of magnitude—the exhaustion of resources, the pollution of the environment, overpopulation, and the possibility of a nuclear holocaust, to mention only four. Physical and biological technologies could, of course, help. We could find new sources of energy and make better use of those we had. The world could feed itself by growing more nutritious grains and eating grain rather than meat. More reliable methods of contraception could keep the population within bounds. Impregnable defenses could make a nuclear war impossible. But that would happen only if human behavior changed, and how it could be changed was still an unanswered question. How were people to be induced to use new forms of energy, to eat grain rather than meat, and to limit the size of their families; and how were atomic stockpiles to be kept out of the hands of desperate leaders?

From time to time policy makers in high places have been urged to pay more attention to the behavioral sciences. The National Research Council, the operative arm of the National Academy of Sciences, made one such proposal a number of years ago, pointing out that useful "insights in policy formulation" had been developed. But it implied that the chief role of the behavioral sciences was to collect facts and insisted, possibly to reassure policy makers who might be alarmed by the ambitions of scientists, that "knowledge is no substitute for wisdom or common sense in making decisions." Science would get the facts but Congress or the President would make the decisions—with wisdom and common sense.

It is true that when the behavioral sciences have gone beyond the collection of facts to recommend courses of action and have done so by predicting consequences, they have not been too helpful. Not all economists agree, for example, on how an increase or reduction in taxes or a change in interest rates will affect business, prices, or unemployment, and political scientists are no more likely to agree on the consequences of domestic or international policies. In anthropology, sociology, and psychology the preferred formulations are those that do not dictate action. A thoroughgoing developmentalism, for example, almost denies the possibility of effective action. Applied psychology is usually a mixture of science and common sense, and Freud regarded therapy as a minor contribution of psychoanalysis.

From the very beginning the application of an experimental analysis of behavior was different. It was doubly concerned with consequences. Behavior could be changed by changing its consequences—that was operant conditioning—but it could be changed because other kinds of consequences would then follow. Psychotic and retarded persons would lead better lives, time and energy of teachers and students would be saved, homes would be pleasanter social environments, people would work more effectively while enjoying what they were doing, and so on.

These are the kinds of achievements traditionally expected from wisdom and common sense, but Frazier, the protagonist of *Walden Two,* insists that they are within reach of a special behavioral science which can take the place of wisdom and common sense and with happier results. And what has happened in the past twenty-five years has increased the plausibility of his achievement— a community in which the most important problems of daily life, as well as certain aspects of economics and government, are solved.

Frazier's critics will protest. What can we conclude from a successful community of a thousand people? Try those principles on New York City, say, or on the State Department and see what happens. The world is a vast and complex space. What works for a small group will be far short of what is needed for a nation or the world as a whole.

Frazier might answer by calling Walden Two a pilot experiment. Industries do not invest in large plants until they have tried a new process on a smaller scale. If we want to find out how people can live together without quarreling, can produce the goods they need without working too hard, or can raise and educate their children more efficiently, let us start with units of manageable size before moving on to larger problems.

But a more cogent answer is this: what is so wonderful about being big? It is often said that the world is suffering from the ills of bigness, and we now have some clinical examples in our large cities. Many cities are probably past the point of good government because too many things are wrong. Should we not rather ask whether we need cities? With modern systems of communication and transportation, businesses do not need to be within walking or taxicab distances of each other, and how many people must one be near in order to live a happy life? People who flock to cities looking for jobs and more interesting lives will flock back again if jobs and more interesting lives are to be found where they came from. It has been suggested that, with modern systems of communication, the America of the future may be simply a network of small towns. But should we not say Walden Twos? A few skeletons of cities may survive, like the bones of dinosaurs in museums, as the remains of a passing phase in the evolution of a way of life.

The British economist E. F. Schumacher, in his remarkable book *Small Is Beautiful*,[2] has discussed the problems that come from bigness and has outlined a technology appropriate to systems of intermediate size. Many current projects dealing with new sources of energy and new forms of agriculture seem ideally suited to development by small communities. A network of small towns or Walden Twos would have its own problems, but the astonishing fact is that it could much more easily solve many of the crucial problems facing the world today. Although a small community does not bring out "human nature in all its essential goodness" (small towns have never supported that romantic dream), it makes it possible to arrange more effective "contingencies of reinforcement" according to the principles of an applied behavior analysis. We need not look too closely at practices derived from such principles to survey some of those which could solve basic problems in a small community.

[2] Schumacher, E. F. *Small Is Beautiful*. New York: Harper Torchbooks, 1973.

To induce people to adapt to new ways of living which are less consuming and hence less polluting, we do not need to speak of frugality or austerity as if we meant sacrifice. There are contingencies of reinforcement in which people continue to pursue (and even overtake) happiness while consuming far less than they now consume. The experimental analysis of behavior has clearly shown that it is not the quantity of goods that counts (as the law of supply and demand suggests) but the contingent relation between goods and behavior. That is why, to the amazement of the American tourist, there are people in the world who are happier than we are, while possessing far less. Inflation is said to be the most serious problem in the world today. It has been defined, not ineptly, as spending more than one has. In an experimental community contingencies of reinforcement which encourage unnecessary spending can be corrected. As for pollution, small communities are optimal for recycling materials and avoiding wasteful methods of distribution.

The basic research has also shown how important it is for everyone, young and old, women and men, not only to receive goods but to engage in their production. That does mean that we should all work like eager beavers according to the Protestant work ethic. There are many ways of saving labor, but they should not, as Frazier points out, be used to save laborers and hence to increase unemployment. Simply by dividing the total amount of wages Americans receive each year by the number of people who want jobs, we arrive at a perfectly reasonable annual wage for everyone. But that means a reduction in the standard of living for many people, which, as things now stand, is probably impossible. In a series of small communities, however, everyone would have a job because work, as well as wages, could be divided among workers. And good incentive conditions—for example, those in which people make not money, but the things that money buys—do not require what we call hard work.

If the world is to save any part of its resources for the future, it must reduce not only consumption but the number of consumers. It should be easy to change the birthrate in an experimental community. Parents would not need children for economic security, the childless could spend as much time with children as they liked, and the community would function as a large and affectionate family in which everyone would play parental and filial roles. Blood ties would then be a minor issue.

People are more likely to treat each other with friendship and affection if they are not in competition for personal or professional status. But good personal relations also depend upon immediate signs of commendation or censure, supported perhaps by simple rules or codes. The bigness of a large city is troublesome precisely because we meet so many people whom we shall never see again and whose commendation or censure is therefore meaningless. The problem cannot really be solved by delegating censure to a police force and the law courts. Those who have used behavior modification in family counseling or in institutions know how to arrange the face-to-face conditions which promote interpersonal respect and love.

We could solve many of the problems of delinquency and crime if we could change the early environment of offenders. One need not be a bleeding heart to argue that many young people today have simply not been prepared by their homes or school to lead successful lives within the law or, if prepared, do not have the chance to do so by getting jobs. Offenders are seldom improved by being sent to prison, and judges therefore tend to reduce or suspend sentences, but crime, unpunished, then increases. We all know how early environments can be improved, and a much-neglected experiment reported by Cohen and Filipczak [3] has demonstrated that occasional offenders can be rehabilitated.

Children are our most valuable resources and they are now shamefully wasted. Wonderful things can be done in the first years of life, but we leave them to people whose mistakes range all the way from child abuse to overprotection and the lavishing of affection on the wrong behavior. We give small children little chance to develop good relationships with their peers or with adults, especially in the single-parent home, which is on the increase. That is all changed when children are, from the very first, part of a larger community.

City schools show how much harm bigness can do to education, and education is important because it is concerned with the

[3] Cohen, H. L., and Filipczak, J. *A New Learning Environment.* San Francisco: Jossey-Bass, 1971.

transmission and hence the survival of a culture. We know how to solve many educational problems with programmed instruction and good contingency management, saving resources and the time and effort of teachers and students. Small communities are ideal settings for new kinds of instruction, free from interference by administrators, politicians, and organizations of teachers.

In spite of our lip service to freedom, we do very little to further the development of the individual. How many Americans can say that they are doing the kinds of things they are best qualified to do and most enjoy doing? What opportunities have they had to choose fields related to their talents or to the interests and skills they acquired in early life? Women, only just beginning to be able to choose not to be housewives, can now discover how hard it is to choose the right profession when they are young or to change to a different one later on.

And once one is lucky enough to be doing what one likes, what are the chances of being successful? How easily can artists, composers, and writers bring their work to the attention of those who will enjoy it and whose reactions will shape behavior in creative ways? Those who know the importance of contingencies of reinforcement know how people can be led to discover the things they do best and the things from which they will get the greatest satisfaction.

Although sometimes questioned, the survival value of art, music, literature, games, and other activities not tied to the serious business of life is clear enough. A culture must positively reinforce the behavior of those who support it and must avoid creating negative reinforcers from which its members will escape through defection. A world which has been made beautiful and exciting by artists, composers, writers, and performers is as important for survival as one which satisfies biological needs.

The effective use of leisure is almost completely neglected in modern life. We boast of our short workday and week, but what we do with the free time we have to spend is nothing of which we can be very proud. The leisure classes have almost always turned to alcohol and other drugs, to gambling, and to watching other people lead exhausting or dangerous lives, and we are no exception. Thanks to television millions of Americans now lead the exciting and dangerous lives of other people. Many states are legalizing gambling and have set up lotteries of their own. Alcohol and drugs are consumed in ever-increasing quantities. One may spend one's life in these ways and be essentially unchanged at the end of it. These uses of leisure are due to some basic behavioral processes, but the same processes, in a different environment, lead people to develop their skills and capacities to the fullest possible extent.

Are we quite sure of all this? Perhaps not, but Walden Two can help us make sure. Even as part of a larger design, a community serves as a pilot experiment. The question is simply whether it works, and one way or the other, the answer is usually clear. When that is the case, we can increase our understanding of human behavior with the greatest possible speed. Here is possibly our best chance to answer the really important questions facing the world today—questions not about economics or government but about the daily lives of human beings.

Yes, but what about economics and government? Must we not answer those questions too? I am not sure we must. Consider the following economic propositions. The first is from Henry David Thoreau's *Walden:* by reducing the amount of goods we consume, we can reduce the amount of time we spend in unpleasant labor. The second appears to assert just the opposite: we must all consume as much as possible so that everyone can have a job. I submit that the first is more reasonable, even though the second is defended by many people today. Indeed, it might be argued that if America were to convert to a network of small communities, our economy would be wrecked. But something is wrong when it is the system that must be saved rather than the way of life that the system is supposed to serve.

But what about government? Surely I am not suggesting that we can get along without a federal government? But how much of it is needed? One great share of our national budget goes to the Department of Health, Education and Welfare. Health? Education? Welfare? But an experimental community like Walden Two *is* health, education, and welfare! The only reason we have a vast federal department is that millions of people find themselves trapped in overgrown, unworkable living spaces.

Another large share of the budget goes to the Department of Defense. Am I suggesting that we can get along without that? How can we preserve the peace of the world if we do not possess the most powerful weapons, together with an industry that continues to develop even more powerful ones? But we have weapons only because other countries have them, and although we feel threatened by countries with comparable military power, particularly the Bomb, the real threat may be the countries that have next to nothing. A few highly industrialized nations cannot long continue to face the rest of the world while consuming and polluting the environment as they do. A way of life in which each person used only a fair share of the resources of the world and yet somehow enjoyed life would be a real step toward world peace. It is a pattern that could easily be copied, and I was heartened recently when someone from the State Department called to tell me that he thought America ought to stop trying to export the "American way of life" and export Walden Twos instead. A state defined by repressive, formal, legal, social controls based on physical force is not necessary in the development of civilization,[4] and although such a state has certainly figured in our own development, we may be ready to move on to another stage.

Suppose we do know what is needed for the good life; how are we to bring it about? In America we almost instinctively move to change things by political action: we pass laws, we vote for new leaders. But a good many people are beginning to wonder. They have lost faith in a democratic process in which the so-called will of the people is obviously controlled in undemocratic ways. And there is always the question whether a government based on punitive sanctions is inappropriate if we are to solve problems nonpunitively.

It has been argued that the solution might be socialism, but it has often been pointed out that socialism, like capitalism, is committed to growth, and hence to overconsumption and pollution. Certainly Russia after fifty years is not a model we wish to emulate. China may be closer to the solutions I have been talking about, but a Communist revolution in America is hard to imagine. It would be a bloody affair, and there is always Lenin's question to be answered: How much suffering can one impose upon those now living for the sake of those who will follow? And can we be sure that those who follow will be any better off?

[4] See Service, Elman. *Origins of the State and Civilization.* New York: Norton, 1975.

Fortunately, there is another possibility. An important theme in *Walden Two* is that political action is to be avoided. Historians have stopped writing about wars and conquering heroes and empires, and what they have turned to instead, though far less dramatic, is far more important. The great cultural revolutions have not started with politics. The great men who are said to have made a difference in human affairs—Confucius, Buddha, Jesus, the scholars and scientists of the Revival of Learning, the leaders of the Enlightenment, Marx—were not political leaders. They did not change history by running for office. We need not aspire to their eminence in order to profit from their example. What is needed is not a new political leader or a new kind of government but further knowledge about human behavior and new ways of applying that knowledge to the design of cultural practices.

It is now widely recognized that great changes must be made in the American way of life. Not only can we not face the rest of the world while consuming and polluting as we do, we cannot for long face ourselves while acknowledging the violence and chaos in which we live. The choice is clear: either we do nothing and allow a miserable and probably catastrophic future to overtake us, or we use our knowledge about human behavior to create a social environment in which we shall live productive and creative lives and do so without jeopardizing the chances that those who follow us will be able to do the same. Something like a Walden Two would not be a bad start.

PART II

THE SCIENCE
OF
BEHAVIOR

6 *The Steep and Thorny Way to a Science of Behavior*

7 *Can We Profit from Our Discovery of Behavioral Science?*

8 *Why I Am Not a Cognitive Psychologist*

9 *The Experimental Analysis of Behavior (A History)*

6

The Steep and Thorny Way
to a Science of Behavior

A critic contends that a recent book of mine [1] does not contain anything new, that much the same was said more than four centuries ago in theological terms by John Calvin. You will not be surprised, then, to find me commending to you the steep and thorny way to that heaven promised by a science of behavior. But I am not one of those ungracious pastors, of whom Ophelia complained, who "recking not their own rede themselves tread the primrose path of dalliance." No, I shall rail at dalliance, and in a manner worthy, I hope, of my distinguished predecessor. If I do not thunder or fulminate, it is only because we moderns can more easily portray a truly frightening hell. I shall merely allude to the carcinogenic fallout of a nuclear holocaust. And no Calvin ever had better reason to fear his hell, for I am proceeding on the assumption that nothing less than a vast improvement in our understanding of human behavior will prevent the destruction of our way of life or of mankind.

Why has it been so difficult to be scientific about human be-

[1] Skinner, B. F. *Beyond freedom and dignity*. New York: Alfred A. Knopf, 1971.

68

havior? Why have methods that have been so prodigiously successful almost everywhere else failed so ignominiously in this one field?
Is it because human behavior presents unusual obstacles to a
science? No doubt it does, but I think we are beginning to see how
these obstacles may be overcome. The problem, I submit, is digression. We have been drawn off the straight and narrow path, and
the word *diversion* serves me well by suggesting not only digression
but dalliance. In this article I analyze some of the diversions pecu-
liar to the field of human behavior which seem to have delayed our
advance toward the better understanding we desperately need.

I must begin by saying what I take a science of behavior to be.
It is, I assume, part of biology. The organism that behaves is the
organism that breathes, digests, conceives, gestates, and so on. As
such, the behaving organism will eventually be described and explained by the anatomist and physiologist. As far as behavior is
concerned, they will give us an account of the genetic endowment
of the species and tell how that endowment changes during the lifetime of the individual and why, as a result, the individual then
responds in a given way on a given occasion. Despite remarkable
progress, we are still a long way from a satisfactory account in such
terms. We know something about the chemical and electrical effects
of the nervous system and the location of many of its functions, but
the events that actually underlie a single instance of behavior—as a
pigeon picks up a stick to build a nest, or a child a block to complete
a tower, or a scientist a pen to write a paper—are still far out of reach.

Fortunately, we need not wait for further progress of that sort.
We can analyze a given instance of behavior in its relation to the
current setting and to antecedent events in the history of the species
and of the individual. Thus, we do not need an explicit account
of the anatomy and physiology of genetic endowment in order to
describe the behavior, or the behavioral processes, characteristic of
a species, or to speculate about the contingencies of survival under
which they might have evolved, as the ethologists have convincingly
demonstrated. Nor do we need to consider anatomy and physiology
in order to see how the behavior of the individual is changed by
his exposure to contingencies of reinforcement during his lifetime
and how as a result he behaves in a given way on a given occasion.

I must confess to a predilection here for my own specialty, the experimental analysis of behavior, which is a quite explicit investigation of the effects upon individual organisms of extremely complex and subtle contingencies of reinforcement.

There will be certain temporal gaps in such an analysis. The behavior and the conditions of which it is a function do not occur in close temporal or spatial proximity, and we must wait for physiology to make the connection. When it does so, it will not invalidate the behavioral account (indeed, its assignment could be said to be specified by that account), nor will it make its terms and principles any the less useful. A science of behavior will be needed for both theoretical and practical purposes even when the behaving organism is fully understood at another level, just as much of chemistry remains useful even though a detailed account of a single instance may be given at the level of molecular or atomic forces. Such, then, is the science of behavior from which I suggest we have been diverted—by several kinds of dalliance to which I now turn.

Very little biology is handicapped by the fact that the biologist is himself a specimen of the thing he is studying, but that part of the science with which we are here concerned has not been so fortunate. We seem to have a kind of inside information about our behavior. It may be true that the environment shapes and controls our behavior as it shapes and controls the behavior of other species—but *we* have feelings about it. And what a diversion they have proved to be. Our loves, our fears, our feelings about war, crime, poverty, and God—these are all basic, if not ultimate, concerns. And we are as much concerned about the feelings of others. Many of the great themes of mythology have been about feelings—of the victim on his way to sacrifice or of the warrior going forth to battle. We read what poets tell us about their feelings, and we share the feelings of characters in plays and novels. We follow regimens and take drugs to alter our feelings. We become sophisticated about them in, say, the manner of La Rochefoucauld, noting that jealousy thrives on doubt, or that the clemency of a ruler is a mixture of vanity, laziness, and fear. And along with some psychiatrists we may even try to establish an independent science of feelings in the intrapsychic life of the mind or personality.

And do feelings not have some bearing on our formulation of a science of behavior? Do we not strike because we are angry and play music because we feel like listening? And if so, are our feelings not to be added to those antecedent events of which behavior is a function? This is not the place to answer such questions in detail, but I must at least suggest the kind of answer that may be given. William James questioned the causal order: Perhaps we do not strike because we are angry but feel angry because we strike. That does not bring us back to the environment, however, although James and others were on the right track. What we feel are conditions of our bodies, most of them closely associated with behavior and with the circumstances in which we behave. We both strike *and* feel angry for a common reason, and that reason lies in the environment. In short, the bodily conditions we feel are *collateral products* of our genetic and environmental histories. They have no explanatory force; they are simply additional facts to be taken into account.

Feelings enjoy an enormous advantage over genetic and environmental histories. They are warm, salient, and demanding, where facts about the environment are easily overlooked. Moreover, they are *immediately* related to behavior, being collateral products of the same causes, and have therefore commanded more attention than the causes themselves, which are often rather remote. In doing so, they have proved to be one of the most fascinating attractions along the path of dalliance.

A much more important diversion has, for more than 2,000 years, made any move toward a science of behavior particularly difficult. The environment acts upon an organism at the surface of its body, but when the body is our own, we seem to observe its progress beyond that point; for example, we seem to see the real world become experience, a physical presentation become a sensation or a percept. Indeed, this second stage may be all we see. Reality may be merely an inference and, according to some authorities, a bad one. What is important may not be the physical world on the far side of the skin but what that world means to us on this side.

Not only do we seem to see the environment on its way in, we seem to see behavior on its way out. We observe certain early stages —wishes, intentions, ideas, and acts of will—before they have, as we say, found expression in behavior. And as for our environmental history, that can also be viewed and reviewed inside the skin, for we have tucked it all away in the storehouse of our memory. Again this is not the place to present an alternative account, but several points need to be made. The behavioristic objection is not primarily to the metaphysical nature of mind stuff. I welcome the view, clearly gaining in favor among psychologists and physiologists and by no means a stranger to philosophy, that what we introspectively observe, as well as feel, are states of our bodies. But I am not willing to give introspection much of a toehold even so, for there are two important reasons why we do not discriminate precisely among our feelings and states of mind and hence why there are many different philosophies and psychologies.

In the first place, the world within the skin is private. Only the person whose skin it is can make certain kinds of contact with it. We might expect that the resulting intimacy should make for greater clarity, but there is a difficulty. The privacy interferes with the very process of coming to know. The verbal community which teaches us to make distinctions among things in the world around us lacks the information it needs to teach us to distinguish events in our private world. For example, it cannot teach us the difference between diffidence and embarrassment as readily or as accurately as that between red and blue or sweet and sour.

Second, the self-observation that leads to introspective knowledge is limited by anatomy. It arose very late in the evolution of the species because it is only when a person begins to be asked about his behavior and about why he behaves as he does that he becomes conscious of himself in this sense. Self-knowledge depends on language and in fact on language of a rather advanced kind, but when questions of this sort first began to be asked, the only nervous systems available in answering them were those that had evolved for entirely different reasons. They had proved useful in the internal economy of the organism, in the coordination of movement, and in operating upon the environment, but there was no reason why they should be suitable in supplying information about those very extensive systems that mediate behavior. To put it crudely, introspection cannot be very relevant or comprehensive because the human organism does not have nerves going to the right places.

One other problem concerns the nature and location of the knower. The organism itself lies, so to speak, between the environment that acts upon it and the environment it acts upon, but what lies between those inner stages—between, for example, experience and will? From what vantage point do we watch stimuli on their way into the storehouse of memory or behavior on its way out to physical expression? The observing agent, the knower, seems to contract to something very small in the middle of things.

In the formulation of a science with which I began, it is the *organism as a whole* that behaves. It acts in and upon a physical world, and it can be induced by a verbal environment to respond to some of its own activities. The events observed as the life of the mind, like feelings, are *collateral products,* which have been made the basis of many elaborate metaphors. The philosopher at his desk asking himself what he really knows, about himself or the world, will quite naturally begin with his experiences, his acts of will, and his memory, but the effort to understand the mind from that vantage point, beginning with Plato's supposed discovery, has been one of the great diversions which have delayed an analysis of the role of the environment.

It did not, of course, take inside information to induce people to direct their attention to what is going on inside the behaving organism. We almost instinctively look inside a system to see how it works. We do this with clocks, as with living systems. It is standard practice in much of biology. Some early efforts to understand and explain behavior in this way have been described by Onians in his classic *Origins of European Thought.*[2] It must have been the slaughterhouse and the battlefield that gave man his first knowledge of anatomy and physiology. The various functions assigned to parts of the organism were not usually those that had been observed introspectively. If Onians is right, the *phrénes* were the lungs, intimately associated with breathing and hence, so the Greeks said,

[2] Onians, R. D. *The origins of European thought.* Cambridge, England: University Press, 1951.

with thought and, of course, with life and death. The *phrénes* were the seat of *thumós,* a vital principle whose nature is not now clearly understood, and possibly of ideas, in the active sense of Homeric Greek. (By the time an idea had become an object of quiet contemplation, interest seems to have been lost in its location.) Later, the various fluids of the body, the humors, were associated with dispositions, and the eye and the ear with sense data. I like to imagine the consternation of that pioneer who first analyzed the optics of the eyeball and realized that the image on the retina was upside down!

Observation of a behaving system from within began in earnest with the discovery of reflexes, but the reflex arc was not only not the seat of mental action, it was taken to be a usurper, the spinal reflexes replacing the *Rückenmarkseele* or soul of the spinal cord, for example. The reflex arc was essentially an anatomical concept, and the physiology remained largely imaginary for a long time. Many years ago I suggested that the letters CNS could be said to stand, not for the central nervous system, but for the conceptual nervous system. I had in mind the great physiologists Sir Charles Sherrington and Ivan Petrovich Pavlov. In his epoch-making *Integrative Action of the Nervous System,* Sherrington [3] had analyzed the role of the synapse, listing perhaps a dozen characteristic properties. I pointed out that he had never seen a synapse in action and that all the properties assigned to it were inferred from the behavior of his preparations. Pavlov had offered his researches as evidence of the activities of the cerebral cortex though he had never observed the cortex in action but had merely inferred its processes from the behavior of his experimental animals. But Sherrington, Pavlov, and many others were moving in the direction of an instrumental approach, and the physiologist is now, of course, studying the nervous system directly.

The conceptual nervous system has been taken over by other disciplines—by information theory, cybernetics, systems analyses, mathematical models, and cognitive psychology. The hypothetical structures they describe do not depend on confirmation by direct observation of the nervous system, for that lies too far in the future

---

[3] Sherrington, C. S. *Integrative action of the nervous system.* New Haven, Conn.: Yale University Press, 1906.

to be of interest. They are to be justified by their internal consistency and the successful prediction of selected facts, presumably not the facts from which the constructions were inferred.

These disciplines are concerned with how the brain or the mind must work if the human organism is to behave as it does. They offer a sort of thermodynamics of behavior without reference to molecular action. The computer with its apparent simulation of Man Thinking supplies the dominant analogy. It is not a question of the physiology of the computer—how it is wired or what type of storage it uses—but of its behavioral characteristics. A computer takes in information as an organism receives stimuli and processes it according to an inbuilt program as an organism is said to do according to its genetic endowment. It encodes the information, converting it to a form it can handle, as the organism converts visual, auditory, and other stimuli into nerve impulses. Like its human analogue it stores the encoded information in a memory, tagged to facilitate retrieval. It uses what it has stored to process information as received, as a person is said to use prior experience to interpret incoming stimuli, and later to perform various operations—in short, to compute. Finally, it makes decisions and behaves: It prints out.

There is nothing new about any of this. The same things were done thousands of years ago with clay tiles. The overseer or tax collector kept a record of bags of grain, the number, quality, and kind being marked appropriately. The tiles were stored in lots as marked, additional tiles were grouped appropriately, the records were eventually retrieved and computations made, and a summary account was issued. The machine is much swifter, and it is so constructed that human participation is needed only before and after the operation. The speed is a clear advantage, but the apparent autonomy has caused trouble. It has seemed to mean that the mode of operation of a computer resembles that of a person. People do make physical records which they store and retrieve and use in solving problems, but it does not follow that they do anything of the sort in the mind. If there were some exclusively subjective achievement, the argument for the so-called higher mental processes would be stronger, but as far as I know, none has been demonstrated. True, we say that the mathematician sometimes intuitively solves a problem and only later, if at all, reduces it to the steps of a proof, and in doing so he seems to differ greatly from those who proceed step by step, but the differences could well be in the evidence of what has happened, and it would not be very satisfactory to define thought simply as unexplained behavior.

Again, it would be foolish of me to try to develop an alternative account in the space available. What I have said about the introspectively observed mind applies as well to the mind that is constructed from observations of the behavior of others. The *accessibility* of stored memories, for example, can be interpreted as the *probability* of acquired behaviors, with no loss in the adequacy of the treatment of the facts, and with a very considerable gain in the assimilation of this difficult field with other parts of human behavior.

I have said that much of biology looks inside a living system for an explanation of how it works. But that is not true of all of biology. Sir Charles Bell could write a book on the hand as evidence of design. The hand was evidence; the design lay elsewhere. Darwin found the design, too, but in a different place. He could catalog the creatures he discovered on the voyage of the *Beagle* in terms of their form or structure, and he could classify barnacles for years in the same way, but he looked beyond structure for the principle of natural selection. It was *the relation of the organism to the environment* that mattered in evolution. And it is the relation to environment that is of primary concern in the analysis of behavior. Hence, it is not enough to confine oneself to organization or structure, even of the most penetrating kind. That is the mistake of most of phenomenology, existentialism, and the structuralism of anthropology and linguistics. When the important thing is a relation to the environment, as in the phylogeny and ontogeny of behavior, the fascination with an inner system becomes a simple digression.

We have not advanced more rapidly to the methods and instruments needed in the study of behavior precisely because of the diverting preoccupation with a supposed or real inner life. It is true that the introspective psychologist and the model builder have investigated environments, but they have done so only to throw some light on the internal events in which they are interested. They are no doubt well-intentioned helpmates, but they have often simply misled those who undertake the study of the organism as a behaving system in its own right. Even when helpful, an observed or hypothetical inner determiner is no explanation of behavior until it has itself been explained, and the fascination with an inner life has allayed curiosity about the further steps to be taken.

I can hear my critics: "Do you really mean to say that all those who have inquired into the human mind, from Plato and Aristotle through the Romans and Scholastics, to Bacon and Hobbes, to Locke and the other British empiricists, to John Stuart Mill, and to all those who began to call themselves psychologists— that they have all been wasting their time?" Well, not all of their time, fortunately. Forget their purely psychological speculations, and they were still remarkable people. They would have been even more remarkable, in my opinion, if they could have forgotten that speculation themselves. They were careful observers of human behavior, but the intuitive wisdom they acquired from their contact with real people was flawed by their theories.

It is easier to make the point in the field of medicine. Until the present century very little was known about bodily processes in health and disease from which useful therapeutic practices could be derived. Yet it should have been worthwhile to call in a physician. Physicians saw many ill people and should have acquired a kind of wisdom, unanalyzed perhaps but still of value in prescribing simple treatments. The history of medicine, however, is largely the history of barbaric practices—bloodlettings, cuppings, poultices, purgations, violent emetics—which much of the time must have been harmful. My point is that these measures were not suggested by the intuitive wisdom acquired from familiarity with illness; they were suggested by *theories,* theories about what was going on inside an ill person. Theories of the mind have had a similar effect, less dramatic, per- haps, but quite possibly far more damaging. The men I have men- tioned made important contributions in government, religion, ethics, economics, and many other fields. They could do so with an intuitive wisdom acquired from experience. But philosophy and psychology have had their bleedings, cuppings, and purgations too, and they have obscured simple wisdom. They have diverted wise people from a path that would have led more directly to an even- tual science of behavior. Plato would have made far more progress

toward the good life if he could have forgotten those shadows
on the wall of his cave.

Still another kind of concern for the self distracts us from
the program I have outlined. It has to do with the individual, not
as an object of self-knowledge, but as an agent, an initiator, a
creator. I have developed this theme in *Beyond Freedom and Dignity*. We are more likely to give a person credit for what he does if it
is not obvious that it can be attributed to his physical or social
environment, and we are likely to feel that truly great achievements
must be inexplicable. The more derivative a work of art, the less
creative; the more conspicuous the personal gain, the less heroic an
act of sacrifice. To obey a well-enforced law is not to show civic
virtue. We see a concern for the aggrandizement of the individual,
for the maximizing of credit due him, in the self-actualization of so-
called humanistic psychology, in some versions of existentialism, in
Eastern mysticism and certain forms of Christian mysticism in which
a person is taught to reject the world in order to free himself for
union with a divine principle or with God, as well as in the simple
structuralism that looks to the organization of behavior rather than to
the antecedent events responsible for that organization. The difficulty
is that if the credit due a person is infringed by evidences of the conditions of which his behavior is a function, then a scientific analysis appears to be an attack on human worth or dignity. Its task is to explain
the hitherto inexplicable and hence to reduce any supposed inner
contribution which has served in lieu of explanation. Freud moved in
this direction in explaining creative art, and it is no longer just the
cynic who traces heroism and martyrdom to powerful indoctrina-
tion. The culminating achievement of the human species has been
said to be the evolution of man as a moral animal, but a simpler
view is that it has been the evolution of cultures in which people
behave morally although they have undergone no inner change of
character.

Even more traumatic has been the supposed attack on freedom. Historically, the struggle for freedom has been an escape from
physical restraint and from behavioral restraints exerted through
punishment and exploitative measures of other kinds. The individual has been freed from features of his environment arranged by

governmental and religious agencies and by those who possess great wealth. The success of that struggle, though it is not yet complete, is one of man's great achievements, and no sensible person would challenge it. Unfortunately, one of its by-products has been the slogan that "all control of human behavior is wrong and must be resisted." Nothing in the circumstances under which man has struggled for freedom justifies this extension of the attack on controlling measures, and we should have to abandon all of the advantages of a well-developed culture if we were to relinquish all practices involving the control of human behavior. Yet new techniques in education, psychotherapy, incentive systems, penology, and the design of daily life are currently subject to attack because they are said to threaten personal freedom, and I can testify that the attack can be fairly violent.

The extent to which a person is free or responsible for his achievements is not an issue to be decided by rigorous proof, but I submit that what we call the behavior of the human organism is no more free than its digestion, gestation, immunization, or any other physiological process. Because it involves the environment in many subtle ways it is much more complex, and its lawfulness is, therefore, much harder to demonstrate. But a scientific analysis moves in that direction, and we can already throw some light on traditional topics, such as free will or creativity, which is more helpful than traditional accounts, and I believe that further progress is imminent.

The issue is, of course, determinism. Slightly more than 100 years ago, in a famous paper, Claude Bernard raised with respect to physiology the issue which now stands before us in the behavioral sciences. The almost insurmountable obstacle to the application of scientific method in biology was, he said, the belief in "vital spontaneity." His contemporary, Louis Pasteur, was responsible for a dramatic test of the theory of spontaneous generation, and I suggest that the spontaneous generation of behavior in the guise of ideas and acts of will is now at the stage of the spontaneous generation of life in the form of maggots and microorganisms 100 years ago.

The practical problem in continuing the struggle for freedom and dignity is not to destroy controlling forces but to change them, to create a world in which people will achieve far more than they have ever achieved before in art, music, literature, science, technology, and above all the enjoyment of life. It could be a world in which people feel freer than they have ever felt before, because they will not be under aversive control. In building such a world, we shall need all the help a science of behavior can give us. To misread the theme of the struggle for freedom and dignity and to relinquish all efforts to control would be a tragic mistake.

But it is a mistake that may very well be made. Our concern for the individual as a creative agent is not dalliance; it is clearly an obstacle rather than a diversion, for ancient fears are not easily allayed. A shift in emphasis from the individual to the environment, particularly to the social environment, is reminiscent of various forms of totalitarian statism. It is easy to turn from what may seem like an inevitable movement in that direction and to take one's chances with libertarianism. But much remains to be analyzed in that position. For example, we may distinguish between liberty and license by holding to the right to do as we please provided we do not infringe upon similar rights of others, but in doing so we conceal or disguise the public sanctions represented by private rights. Rights and duties, like a moral or ethical sense, are examples of hypothetical internalized environmental sanctions.

In the long run, the aggrandizement of the individual jeopardizes the future of the species and the culture. In effect, it infringes the so-called rights of billions of people still to be born, in whose interests only the weakest of sanctions are now maintained. We are beginning to realize the magnitude of the problem of bringing human behavior under the control of a projected future, and we are already suffering from the fact that we have come very late to recognize that mankind will have a future only if it designs a *viable* way of life. I wish I could share the optimism of both Darwin and Herbert Spencer that the course of evolution is necessarily toward perfection. It appears, on the contrary, that that course must be corrected from time to time. But if the intelligent behavior that corrects it is also a product of evolution, then perhaps they were right after all. But it could be a near thing.

Perhaps it is now clear what I mean by diversions and obstacles. The science I am discussing is the investigation of the relation between behavior and the environment—on the one hand, the environment in which the species evolved and which is responsible for the facts investigated by the ethologists and, on the other hand, the environment in which the individual lives and in response to which at any moment he behaves. We have been diverted from, and blocked in, our inquiries into the relations between behavior and those environments by an absorbing interest in the organism itself. We have been misled by the almost instinctive tendency to look inside any system to see how it works, a tendency doubly powerful in the case of behavior because of the apparent inside information supplied by feelings and introspectively observed states. Our only recourse is to leave that subject to the physiologist, who has, or will have, the only appropriate instruments and methods. We have also been encouraged to move in a centripetal direction because the discovery of controlling forces in the environment has seemed to reduce the credit due us for our achievements and to suggest that the struggle for freedom has not been as fully successful as we had imagined. We are not yet ready to accept the fact that the task is to change, not people, but rather the world in which they live.

We shall be less reluctant to abandon these diversions and to attack these obstacles, as we come to understand the possibility of a different approach. The role of the environment in human affairs has not, of course, gone unnoticed. Historians and biographers have acknowledged influences on human conduct, and literature has made the same point again and again. The Enlightenment advanced the cause of the individual by improving the world in which he lived—the Encyclopedia of Diderot and D'Alembert was designed to further changes of that sort, and by the nineteenth century the controlling force of the environment was clearly recognized. Bentham and Marx have been called behaviorists, although for them the environment determined behavior only after first determining consciousness, and this was an unfortunate qualification because the assumption of a mediating state clouded the relation between the terminal events.

The role of the environment has become clearer in the present century. Its selective action in evolution has been examined by the ethologists, and a similar selective action during the life of the individual is the subject of the experimental analysis of behavior. In the current laboratory, very complex environments are constructed and their effects on behavior studied. I believe this work offers consoling reassurance to those who are reluctant to abandon traditional formulations. Unfortunately, it is not well known outside the field. Its practical uses are, however, beginning to attract attention. Techniques derived from the analysis have proved useful in other parts of biology—for example, physiology and psychopharmacology—and have already led to the improved design of cultural practices, in programmed instructional materials, contingency management in the classroom, behavioral modification in psychotherapy and penology, and many other fields.

Much remains to be done, and it will be done more rapidly when the role of the environment takes its proper place in competition with the apparent evidences of an inner life. As Diderot put it, nearly 200 years ago, "Unfortunately it is easier and shorter to consult oneself than it is to consult nature. Thus the reason is inclined to dwell within itself." But the problems we face are not to be found in men and women but in the world in which they live, especially in those social environments we call cultures. It is an important and promising shift in emphasis because, unlike the remote fastness of the so-called human spirit, the environment is within reach and we are learning how to change it.

And so I return to the role that has been assigned to me as a kind of twentieth-century Calvin, calling on you to forsake the primrose path of total individualism, of self-actualization, self-adoration, and self-love, and to turn instead to the construction of that heaven on earth which is, I believe, within reach of the methods of science. I wish to testify that, once you are used to it, the way is not so steep or thorny after all.

7

Can We Profit from Our Discovery of Behavioral Science?

Many things are happening today that seem completely sense-less, irrational, insane. The population of many countries has been allowed to reach a point at which two or three bad harvests will mean death by starvation for tens or even hundreds of millions of people. The United States and Russia spend a staggering part of their incomes on the production of military systems which every-one hopes will never be used and will therefore prove to be a total waste. Our supplies of energy and many critical materials are surely running out, but we have done very little to curtail current or future use. The environment grows steadily less habitable.

People have always been thoughtless and short-sighted, but can we continue to excuse ourselves by saying so? The human species has emerged triumphant in a long competition with other species. Its members can acquire behavioral repertoires of a unique and extraordinary complexity. Verbal behavior was perhaps its greatest achievement, and it led to the social environments which have produced art, literature, religion, law, and science. With the technologies of physics and biology the species has solved problems of fantastic difficulty. Yet with respect to its own behavior something always seems to go wrong. It is easy to understand why the question should be asked: "When shall we have the behavioral science and technology we need to solve our problems?"

I believe that that is the wrong question and that we should be asking: "Why do we not use the behavioral science we already have?" Consider the position of an agricultural specialist visiting a developing country. He sees farmers planting varieties of grain which are not best suited to the soil, rainfall, or climate or the most resistant to disease. He sees them using too little fertilizer, or fertilizer of the wrong kind. They are cultivating and harvesting with primitive equipment, and processing and storing food in wasteful ways. If they then ask him, "When shall we have the agricultural science we need to make better use of our land?" must he not reply, "Why are you not using the science which already exists?"

There could be many answers. Special seed, fertilizer, machinery, and storage space are costly. If money is available, those who have it must be convinced that spending it will bring results. New methods often throw people out of work and take control out of the hands of those who have profited from the old. But there is a special kind of explanation that is more important. We have all heard stories of third world farmers who change to new methods while they are being demonstrated only to change back as soon as the would-be reformer leaves. The stories may be apocryphal, but they are easy to believe because people do persist in doing things as they have always done them and the entrenched ways do postpone or block any advance toward something better.

We have no reason to feel superior to those who reject better methods of agriculture, for we are doing much the same thing with respect to behavioral science. The parallel with agriculture breaks down, because I cannot point to any part of the world today in which a behavioral technology flourishes, but recent advances in a science of behavior have led to substantial achievements in the management of human behavior in such special fields as government, industry, schools and colleges, institutions for the care of psychotic and retarded people, and personal and family counseling. I shall not review this work, or try to indicate how extensive it is. I simply want to ask why it is not more widely accepted in the solution of our problems.

Money is again relevant, not because we are poor but because changes have consequences which are essentially economic. And again it is true that those who make the decisions to spend money— for example, in education—are often unaware of what can be done. But the main.obstacle is, again, the entrenchment of old practices— in this case of old ways of thinking about human behavior. Antiquated theories ingrained in our language and our culture stand in the way of promising scientific alternatives.

It is not so much the complexity of human behavior that causes trouble as the traditional practice of looking for explanations inside the behaving person. People are said to act as they do because of their feelings, their states of mind, their intentions, purposes, and plans. They act because they will to act. Their roles in society are reflections of inner selves or personalities.

A science of behavior must look elsewhere. It turns to the environment—the environment that has produced the genetic endowment of the species through natural selection and that now shapes and maintains the repertoire of the individual through another selective process called operant conditioning. By analyzing these two roles of the environment we can begin to understand behavior and, by changing the environment, to modify it.

Evidence of the powerful control exerted by the environment is obtained only through rather subtle scientific practices and is by no means as immediate or as obvious as the evidence that seems to support the traditional view. How we feel—or, more precisely, how our bodies feel to us—is a salient part of the situations in which we take action, and we are therefore likely to regard the feelings as the causes of action. And since we usually assume that when others act as we do, they feel as we feel, it is not surprising that when we want them to act in a given way, we try to make them feel as we feel when doing so. The evidence is convincing because it is familiar, but twenty-five hundred years of speculation about it have not led to a convincing mentalistic (or, to use a vogue word, cognitive) theory, and our practical failures are obvious enough in our present difficulties.

Let us look at some examples in which this abiding concern for an inner explanation has diverted attention from environmental measures which might have brought us closer to solving our problems. A feeling or state of mind familiar to everyone is confidence.

The term is useful in daily communication. As a behaviorist I do not blush to say that I am at this moment possessed of a number of different feelings of confidence, and I shall list a few in order of degree. I have complete confidence that this chair and desk will hold me as I write. I have a fair degree of confidence that the words I am writing will eventually reach readers. I have some confidence that a number of those who start reading will finish the paper, and just a touch of confidence that some of them will come to behave in a slightly different way because of what they read. I thus report certain conditions of my own body. But I hasten to point out that the degree of my confidence is related to the extent of my past successes and failures. Similar desks and chairs have always held me. Similar writing has usually been published. A good many readers finish my papers, and readers sometimes change their behavior because of what I write. I am writing a paper at my desk at this moment because I have done much the same kind of thing with some success on fairly similar occasions. For the same reasons I have certain feelings of confidence. But I am writing because of the consequences, not because of the feelings. My feelings and my behavior are collateral products of my personal history.

The point is important when the word is used in discussing practical affairs. The Bulletin of the Royal Society of Arts in London recently reported the remarks of a speaker who had discussed the appearance of the British countryside. He had told his audience that "the key to the survival of our present landscape lay in the word 'confidence'—without which people would not plant trees." In the past year or two, he said, "confidence had been completely destroyed." But the important fact was simply that people no longer planted trees. Why did they not do so? It is not difficult to point to relevant facts. People move about a great deal these days, and when they do so they never watch a tree they have planted grow to maturity. Trees are likely to be wantonly destroyed as new roads are put through and properties broken up for housing developments. More people now live in cities where the government plants the trees. Surely changes of this sort are the real key to the survival of a landscape. They make it less likely that people will plant trees, but why should we say that they first destroy confidence in tree planting? Confidence is not a key to anything.

In the United States there is a Conference Board which reports on "Consumer Confidence in the Economy." A recent decline in its index was called the "first significant sag in consumer spirits since 1974." What the board had discovered was simply that Americans were planning to buy fewer cars, television sets, and so on. Why attribute this to a decline in "confidence" let alone "sagging spirits"? The board made the helpful suggestion that "the major culprit may be inflation." People plan to buy less when their money does not go as far, and when, as a collateral effect, they also lack a feeling of confidence. A move to "restore confidence in the economy" is really a move to encourage buying. The government may, for example, give people more money—say, by reducing taxes—and they are then more likely to buy things.

In speaking of planting trees or buying television sets, the term confidence may simply refer to the likelihood that a person will act in a particular way. Perhaps the feeling is not really meant to be an explanation. But when the behavior cannot be so easily specified, feelings assume a more important role. Confidence begins to be treated as if it really were a cause, and that is when inquiry into valid explanations is obscured.

A year or two ago, in a newsweekly, David E. Lilienthal discussed "the prevailing American mood," which he said "has become negative and fearful." It is "a mood of self-doubt and fear which paralyzes the very will-to-act," and, he added, it is the will-to-act that alone can "remove the causes of fear and lack of confidence." What America needed was more confidence, and Lilienthal offered the Tennessee Valley Authority as an example that proved his point. In the early thirties the soil in the valley of the Tennessee River had lost its fertility, the forests had been almost destroyed, the land was eroding, and nothing much could be done. People were idle and poor. After the dams were built, electric power and fertilizer were available, and the people turned to new methods of agriculture and restored the land. Their incomes rose, and the valley became green. Lilienthal attributes this highly desirable change to "restored self-confidence." But surely it was the dams and their products that made the difference! People began to do things they could not do before, and, being successful, they no doubt felt confident. (Lilienthal cited Iran as another example, and insisted that what was happening there was due to a restoration of a national faith and self-confidence, but a connection with the price of oil is certainly not to be overlooked.)

When we speak of a nation's confidence in itself, the behavior at issue is much more complex than planting trees or buying cars, and we are therefore much more likely to give confidence a power of its own. But if we are content to say that all America needs today is a new spirit of confidence, we shall neglect the things that can actually be done to bring about the changes we desire.

To take confidence one step further, Senator Daniel P. Moynihan recently considered "the contention by some intellectuals here and abroad that democracy is declining as a force in world affairs." World leaders seem to be turning less and less often to democratic processes to solve their problems. The *London Times* made much the same point in a recent issue: "The great democracies are themselves partly losing faith in democracy . . . the United States, which fifteen years ago was still the dominant world power, is now only one of the super-powers, the stronger but in important ways *the less self-confident* of the two" (emphasis added). And a national poll reports that public confidence in our institutions—including the Congress, the executive branch of the federal government, and corporations—has sunk to its lowest point since the poll began to be taken. And so, Senator Moynihan says, "We ask ourselves . . . whether hope is not fading and whether it will not continue to fade unless there is some restoration of confidence and will on our part."

But how can one restore confidence in the democratic process? The President cannot ask drug companies to prepare millions of injections of confidence—like so many inoculations for influenza. We want people to discuss issues, work for candidates, and go to the polls, but they will do so, not because they have confidence in the democratic process, but because certain kinds of consequences then follow. Potential voters stay home when they have nothing to show for their trouble. Voting for the candidate who lost the 1972 presidential election was not, as we say, reinforced, nor, as it turned out, was voting for Nixon, the candidate who won. The behavior of working for, giving to, and voting for a candidate for President underwent a well-known process called, if I may be technical, extinction. To reverse it we need to make sure that the political behavior of the citizen will again have reinforcing consequences. The democratic process works when it makes a difference whether people participate or not.

Confidence is only one of hundreds of terms referring to feelings or states of mind which come to us naturally and conveniently in daily discussions of human behavior but which by their very nature are inimical to a scientific approach. Perhaps no single instance causes serious trouble, because more productive measures are taken when important consequences are at stake, but the general practice of thinking about behavior in this way discourages inquiry into the role of the environment, and explains, I believe, why we are still in such trouble.

The difficulty is compounded by the fact that behavioral scientists themselves are often not free of the old tendencies. Many established concepts suffer from the same shortcomings. In its psychological use, the term *attitude* is an example. It may have begun as a metaphor. Since things usually fall in the direction in which they are leaning, we say that a person leans toward one political candidate or another. To be inclined to do something is also to be in an attitude slightly off the perpendicular. But at some point the term began to refer to an internal state. A distinguished economist, Sir Arthur Lewis, tells us that "economic growth depends on attitudes to work, to wealth, to thrift, to having children, to invention, to strangers, to adventure." He could just as well have said that economic growth depends on whether people work, acquire wealth, save, have children, invent things, get along with strangers, and explore the world. Should we then say that by "attitude" he simply means the likelihood that people will behave in these ways? No, Sir Arthur forgoes that chance of exculpation, for he continues, "and all these attitudes flow from deep springs in the human mind." For him attitudes are more than probabilities of action; they are mental forces. People work, save, spend, bear children, and so on because of their attitudes. If that is so, we can account for economic growth only by looking into the human mind, but we should then look away from the external circumstances about which something can be done—the economic conditions under which people work, acquire goods, and save, and the social

conditions under which they have families and treat each other
well or badly. By speaking of attitudes we draw attention away
from the role of the environment in economic growth.

Another feeling or state of mind with a secure place in social
science is alienation. Workers on a production line complain of
being unhappy, they often stay away from work, and they frequently strike or quit. They are said to do so because, among other
things, they are alienated. Should we not then study what alienation
feels like? The contribution of one authority in the field has been
described as follows: "[He] does not deny that the causes of alienation lie elsewhere, outside of the individual; either in the environment, or in the relation individual-environment. But he does well
to insist on alienation itself as a subjective state of an individual,
to be distinguished sharply from alienating social structures.
Having made this distinction, it can then become a matter of argument whether one should concentrate primarily on alienation itself
[as a subjective state] or on alienating conditions in the social
structure; on the phenomenon itself or on its causes." But the
all-important effect is then ignored. The problem arises because
certain social structures lead people to behave in certain ways; they
may also generate feelings, but that is a collateral effect.

Feelings and states of mind may usurp this role in the causation of behavior mainly because we respond to our own bodies
while we are responding to the world around us, but there are
other reasons. As Freud pointed out, we often act without having
relevant feelings, in which case we should look for other causes.
But Freud is probably responsible for the fact that we look in the
wrong place—deep in a person's mental life. He made a great deal
of the depth of psychoanalysis, as linguists do of deep structures,
and this sense of probing makes a behavioral analysis seem superficial and the appeal to feelings especially profound. A discussion
of the human rights movement in Russia contains the following
question: "Can the consciousness of the Soviet citizenry, and of the
Soviet bureaucracy, be brought to the point where the one demands, and the other provides, the rule of law?" What is "consciousness" doing there? Why not say simply, "Can Soviet citizens be
induced to demand, and the Soviet bureaucracy to provide, the rule
of law?" With the term *consciousness* the writer alludes to something beyond or beneath the behavior itself. And indeed something

beyond the behavior does need to be taken into account—but in certain governmental and social systems, rather then deeply rooted feelings.

I recently received a letter that began: "Have you ever thought about the great reservoir of feeling against war that exists throughout the world? It is being wasted! Bottled up, with nothing to show for it in terms of progress towards real peace . . . let us release this great reservoir of feeling." We all know what the writer is talking about. We read the newspapers and watch news reports on television and are moved to act, but we find there is little we can do. It does seem as if something having to do with war is indeed "bottled up," and that it would be wonderful if we, and millions like us, could pull the cork. But it would be action not feelings that poured out. We should have found something to do to prevent war. But would my correspondent have bothered to write simply to say: "Are you aware of how many people in the world would do something to stop war if they could? Let us give them a chance?" That kind of statement cries out for the response "But how?" If anything can be done, it will be done not by releasing feelings but by specifying the steps to be taken to build a peaceful world. Pent-up feelings and floodgates waiting to be opened are powerful metaphors, but they do not tell us what to do.

A research document published by the International Peace Research Association elaborates upon a famous statement issued by UNESCO many years ago: "Wars begin in the minds of men; hence it is in the minds of men that the defense of peace must be constructed." But how are we to move into the minds of men (and presumably women) and of what are we to construct the defenses of peace? The relevant facts lie in the outside world. Wars begin in many places and for many reasons—overcrowding, competition for world trade, border disputes, concentrations of military power, racial and national claims and counterclaims, the unequal distribution of wealth . . . we know at least some of the things to be done about matters of that sort. Call it a "superficial" analysis if you will, but to turn instead to the minds of men, no matter how deeply implanted they may be, is to abandon any hope of solution.

It is not only a spurious profundity that promotes a mentalistic account. Certain advantages are gained from its weaknesses. Those who must make important decisions suffer when things go wrong. They are held responsible for their action in the sense that they will be punished if they fail. A convenient way to avoid punishment is to call for a change of mind rather than action. Thus, to say that America needs more of the kind of confidence attributed to the Tennessee Valley Project is safer than to say that America needs more projects of the same kind. No one objects to a call for confidence, but a proposal to build more dams and plants may be harshly received. Similarly, those who call for more confidence in the democratic process are not necessarily ready to support changes in the conduct of elections, in the methods of financing candidates, in lobbying practices, or in any of the other conditions which undermine a democratic system. And many of those who call for new attitudes toward work, thrift, and the family may hesitate to advocate the social changes which would effectively induce people to work, save, and have more or fewer children. It is safe to call for changes in feelings and states of mind precisely because nothing will ever happen for which one can be held responsible.

Feelings play a different and possibly more destructive role when they are taken, not as causes, but as values, not as preceding behavior but following it. Nutritious food is essential to the survival of the individual; is it not therefore extremely important that it taste good? Sexual behavior is essential to the survival of the species; is it not extremely important that sexual contact feel good? But the important thing for the individual and the species is not how things taste or feel but whether they are reinforcing—that is, whether they strengthen the behavior upon which they are contingent. Susceptibilities to reinforcement have presumably evolved because of their survival value. When, through a mutation, an organism's behavior is more strongly reinforced by nutritious food or sexual contact, the organism is more likely to get the food it needs and to have offspring. The increased susceptibility to reinforcement is then contributed to the species. The important thing is that the susceptibility should survive. The feelings are incidental.

The same thing is true of the social reinforcers, which are more likely to be called values. People are said to treat each other in ways which express compassion and love and which inspire gratitude, but the important thing is the contribution to the functioning of the social environment or culture. The behavior we call ethical makes a group function more effectively. The feelings or states of mind associated with it are collateral products.

Happiness is a feeling often taken as a value. We struggle to achieve happiness, but an inquiry into how it feels to be happy may not help. On the contrary, it may make the struggle less successful. We often feel happy when we behave in ways leading to the possession of goods, and we then mistakenly take the possession to be the cause of the feeling. We make the same mistake when we act to make others happy by giving them good things. Whole philosophies of government have been tested on the theory that if goods are distributed "to each according to his need" people will be happy. But happiness is the accompaniment of successful action rather than of what the action brings. It is characteristic of getting rather than possessing. Possession leads to happiness only when it makes further action possible. Whether or not people are happy is of great political significance, but a subjective measure of the quality of life will do little more than tell us whether a given change should be made.

Another feeling said to be important as a value is freedom—one of the great human goals and possibly the most important issue in the world today. We gain little from analyzing how it feels to be free; the important things are the conditions under which we do so. When we escape from punishment or the threat of punishment, we say that we are free, and feel free, but we are still under the control of other parts of the environment, particularly the kinds of consequences called positive reinforcement. It is a kind of control under which we do, as we say, what we want to do. We do not try to escape from a world in which such control prevails; on the contrary, we work to preserve it. Nevertheless, as I argue in *Beyond Freedom and Dignity,* the misunderstanding of freedom that comes from a concentration on feelings has actually perpetuated punitive practices and slowed the advance toward a world in which people will feel freer than ever before.

But what about the sheer enjoyment of life—the pleasurable feelings we get from, say, art, music, and literature? Surely the important things here are feelings. But we must not neglect the things we do in enjoying life. We listen to music, look at a picture, read a book, and these are modes of behaving. We stop listening and looking when we do not, as we say, enjoy the consequences. We call some of the things we continue to look at or listen to beautiful, but we could as well say reinforcing. We listen again and again to music we find beautiful, we look again and again at a picture we find beautiful. A study which confined itself to beautiful things, or to how beautiful things made us feel, would not tell us how to explore the world in order to find or create more of them. Nor would it tell us why we are less likely to defect from a group and more likely to defend it and improve it if many things about it are reinforcing in the ways we call beautiful.

And so, in general, we enjoy life and call the world beautiful and ourselves free and happy when our behavior leads to an abundance of good things. No structural account of the things themselves or any analysis of the feelings which arise when behavior is strengthened by them will help us make life more enjoyable and ourselves freer and happier. We must turn instead to the contingent relations between behavior and its consequences.

Such a program does not rob people of their feelings. It simply puts feelings in their proper place, and in doing so moves more rapidly to the kind of environment in which they can be enjoyed. In refusing to accept feelings and states of mind as causes, we do not make the behavior that is said to follow from them any the less important. Instead we make it possible to deal with behavior more successfully.

It is clear that the behavioral sciences have not yet fulfilled their promise. There are economists who question whether there is a science of economics, and if we can judge by international strategies in the world today, governments make little use of political science. Anthropologists, sociologists, and social psychologists grow increasingly uneasy about their fields. (One writer has said that sociology is suffering from a "crisis of confidence!") In most of these fields there is no shortage of facts, and efforts are continually made to discover meaningful relations among them, mathematical or otherwise. What is missing is a coherent theory of human behavior.

The fault lies, I am arguing, with a surviving mentalism. The sooner we abandon explanations of behavior in terms of feelings and states of mind the sooner we shall turn to the genetic and environmental conditions of which behavior is a function. Enough is already known about those conditions to assure reasonable success in the interpretation, prediction, and control of human behavior. A refusal to take advantage of what is within reach could mean the difference between the survival and the destruction of our civilization or even the species.

There are those who will say that such a cause is surely incommensurate with such an effect. A mentalistic philosophy is rather inoffensive, and it need not seriously handicap practical people. Am I not exaggerating its importance? But there must be some reason why we are not making the technological advances in the management of human behavior which are so obvious in other fields, and the reason could be our lingering commitment to the individual as an initiating agent. It is of the very nature of human behavior that seemingly trivial causes have profound effects, and there is a historical example which I am inclined to take seriously. I am not a historian nor do I usually trust arguments based upon history but in this instance the evidence is, I think, persuasive.

From the fifth century B.C. to about 1400 A.D. China was as advanced in physical technology as any part of the world. The recent exhibition of early Chinese pottery and ceramic and bronze sculptures sent around the world by the Chinese government shows an art and a technology fully equal to those of the Greeks of the same period. A comparable position was maintained for nearly two thousand years. Then three great Chinese inventions—the compass, gunpowder, and moveable type—brought about extraordinary change. But not in China! Gunpowder was of little practical use because Chinese military activities were ceremonial and largely under the control of astrologers. Long sea voyages were forbidden, and coastwise shipping gained little from the compass. The Chinese system of notation, with its thousands of characters, could not take advantage of moveable type. It was the West which seized upon these three great Chinese inventions and exploited them with extraordinary results. With the compass the West explored the world and with gunpowder conquered it. Moveable type and the printing press brought the revival of learning and the spread of Western thought. And while all this was happening, China re-

mained a medieval society.[1] Certain rather inoffensive cultural practices had deprived it of the benefit of its own discoveries.

Is it possible that something of the same sort is happening
again, and that this time Western culture will suffer from essentially
ceremonial, astrological, and geomantic practices? Will China, fortunately untouched by the Greek "discovery of the mind," now take
over the behavioral equivalents of compass, gunpowder, and moveable type and dominate a new era? Or is it not too late? Can we
begin at last to profit from our discovery of behavioral science and
use it to share in the solution of the problems facing the world
today? That is the question.

---

[1] McNeill, William. *The rise of the west.* Chicago: University of
Chicago Press, 1963.

8

Why I Am Not
a Cognitive Psychologist

The variables of which human behavior is a function lie in the environment. We distinguish between (1) the selective action of that environment during the evolution of the species, (2) its effect in shaping and maintaining the repertoire of behavior which converts each member of the species into a person, and (3) its role as the occasion upon which behavior occurs. Cognitive psychologists study these relations between organism and environment, but they seldom deal with them directly. Instead they invent internal surrogates which become the subject matter of their science.

Take, for example, the so-called process of association. In Pavlov's experiment a hungry dog hears a bell and is then fed. If this happens many times, the dog begins to salivate when it hears the bell. The standard mentalistic explanation is that the dog "associates" the bell with the food. But it was Pavlov who associated them! "Associate" means to join or unite. The dog merely begins to salivate upon hearing the bell. We have no evidence that it does so because of an internal surrogate of the contingencies.

In the "association of ideas" the ideas are internal replicas of stimuli to which I shall return. If we have eaten lemons, we may taste lemon upon seeing a lemon or see a lemon upon tasting lemon juice, but we do not do this because *we* associate the flavor with the appearance. They are associated in the lemon. "Word associations" are at least correctly named. If we say "home" when someone says "house," it is not because we associate the two words but because they are associated in daily English usage. Cognitive association is an invention. Even if it were real, it would go no further toward an explanation than the external contingencies upon which it is modeled.

Another example is abstraction. Consider a simple experiment. A hungry pigeon can peck any one of a number of panels bearing the names of colors—"white," "red," "blue," and so on, and the pecks are reinforced with small amounts of food. Any one of a number of objects—blocks, books, flowers, toy animals, and so on—can be seen in an adjacent space. The following contingencies are then arranged: whenever the object is white, no matter what its shape or size, pecking only the panel marked "white" is reinforced; whenever the object is red, pecking only the panel marked "red" is reinforced; and so on. Under these conditions the pigeon eventually pecks the panel marked "white" when the object is white, the panel marked "red" when the object is red, and so on. Children are taught to name colors with similar contingencies, and we all possess comparable repertoires sustained by the reinforcing practices of our verbal environments.

But what is said to be going on in the mind? Karl Popper [1] has put a classical issue this way: "We can say either that (1) the universal term "white" is a label attached to a set of things, or that (2) we collect the set because they share an intrinsic property of "whiteness." Popper says the distinction is important; natural scientists may take the first position but social scientists must take the second. Must we say, then, that the pigeon is either attaching a universal term to a set of things or collecting a set of things because they share an intrinsic property? Clearly, it is the *experimenter* not the pigeon who "attaches" the white key to the white objects displayed and who collects the set of objects on which a single reinforcing event is made contingent. Should we not simply

[1] Popper, K. *Poverty of historicism.* London, 1957.

attribute the behavior to the experimental contingencies? And if so, why not for children or ourselves? Behavior comes under the control of stimuli under certain contingencies of reinforcement. Special contingencies maintained by verbal communities produce "abstractions." We do attach physical labels to physical things and we collect physical objects according to labeled properties, but comparable cognitive processes are inventions which, even if real, would be no closer to an explanation than the external contingencies.

Another cognitive account of the same data would assert that a person, if not a pigeon, forms an abstract *idea* or develops a *concept* of color. The development of concepts is an especially popular cognitive field. (The horticultural metaphor minimizes contributions from the environment. We may hasten the growth of the mind but we are no more responsible for its final character than farmers for the character of the fruits and vegetables they so carefully nourish.) Color vision is part of the genetic endowment of most people, and it develops or grows in a physiological sense, possibly to some extent after birth. Nevertheless, most stimuli acquire control because of their place in contingencies of reinforcement. As the contingencies become more complex, they shape and maintain more complex behavior. It is the environment that develops, not a mental or cognitive possession.

A passage from a recent discussion of the development of sexual identity in a child might be translated as follows: "The child forms a concept based upon what it has observed and been told of what it means to be a boy or girl." (A child's behavior is affected by what it has observed and been told about being a boy or girl.) "This concept is oversimplified, exaggerated, and stereotyped." (The contingencies affecting the behavior are simplified and exaggerated and involve stereotyped behavior on the part of parents and others.) "As the child develops cognitively, its concepts, and consequently its activities, become more sophisticated and realistic." (As the child grows older, the contingencies become more subtle and more closely related to the actual sex of the child.) Children do not go around forming concepts of their sexual identity and "consequently" behaving in special ways; they slowly change their behavior as people change the ways in which they treat them because of their sex. Behavior changes because the contingencies change, not because a mental entity called a concept develops.

Many mentalistic or cognitive terms refer not only to contingencies but to the behavior they generate. Terms like "mind," "will," and "thought" are often simply synonyms of "behavior." A historian writes: "What may be called a stagnation of thought prevailed, as though the mind, exhausted after building up the spiritual fabric of the Middle Ages, had sunk into inertia." Exhaustion is a plausible metaphor when a quiet period follows an active one, but it was behavior that became stagnant and inert, presumably because the contingencies changed. Certain social conditions ("the spiritual fabric of the Middle Ages") made people active. A second set of conditions, possibly produced by the very behavior generated by the first, made them much less so. To understand what actually happened we should have to discover why the contingencies changed, not why thought became stagnant or inert.

Behavior is internalized as mental life when it is too slight to be observed by others—when, as we say, it is covert. A writer has pointed out that "the conductor of an orchestra maintains a certain even beat according to an internal rhythm, and he can divide that beat in half again and again with an accuracy rivaling any mechanical instrument." But is there an *internal* rhythm? Beating time is behavior. Parts of the body often serve as pendulums useful in determining speed, as when the amateur musician beats time with a foot or the rock player with the whole body, but other well-timed behavior must be learned. The conductor beats time steadily because he has learned to do so under rather exacting contingencies of reinforcement. The behavior may be reduced in scale until it is no longer visible to others. It is still sensed by the conductor, but it is a sense of behavior not of time. The history of "man's development of a sense of time" over the centuries is not a matter of cognitive growth but of the invention of clocks, calendars, and ways of keeping records—in other words, of an environment that "keeps time."

When a historian reports that in a given period "a wealthy, brilliant, and traditional governing class lost its will," he is reporting simply that it stopped acting like a wealthy, brilliant, and traditional governing class. Deeper changes are suggested by the term "will" but they are not identified. They could not have been changes in particular people, since the period lasted more than one lifetime. What changed were presumably the conditions affecting the behavior of members of the class. Perhaps they lost their money; perhaps competing classes became more powerful.

Feelings, or the bodily conditions we feel, are commonly taken as the causes of behavior. We go for a walk "because we feel like going." It is surprising how often the futility of such an explanation is recognized. A distinguished biologist, C. H. Waddington,[2] reviewing a book by Tinbergen, writes as follows:

> It is not clear how far he Tinbergen would go along with the argument of one of the most perceptive critical discussions of ethology by Suzanne Langer, who argues that each step in a complex structure of behavior is controlled, not by a hierarchical set of neural centers, but by the immediate feelings of the animal. The animal, she claims, does the next thing in the sequence, not to bring about a useful goal, or even as a move toward an enjoyable consummation, but because it actually feels like doing it at the moment.

Evidently Waddington himself goes along partway with this "perceptive view."

But suppose Langer is right. Suppose animals simply do what they feel like doing? What is the next step in explaining their behavior? Clearly, a science of animal behavior must be replaced or supplemented by a science of animal feelings. It would be as extensive as the science of behavior because there would presumably be a feeling for each act. But feelings are harder to identify and describe than the behavior attributed to them, and we should have abandoned an objective subject matter in favor of one of dubious status, accessible only through necessarily defective channels of introspection. The contingencies would be the same. The feelings and the behavior would have the same causes.

A British statesman recently asserted that the key to crime in the streets was "frustration." Young people mug and rob because they feel frustrated. But why do they feel frustrated? One reason

[2] Waddington, C. H., *New York Review*, February 3, 1974.

may be that many of them are unemployed, either because they do not have the education needed to get jobs or because jobs are not available. To solve the problem of street crime, therefore, we must change the schools and the economy. But what role is played in all this by frustration? Is it the case that when one cannot get a job one feels frustrated and that when one feels frustrated one mugs and robs, or is it simply the case that when one cannot earn money, one is more likely to steal it—and possibly to experience a bodily condition called frustration?

Since many of the events which must be taken into account in explaining behavior are associated with bodily states that can be felt, what is felt may serve as a clue to the contingencies. But the feelings are not the contingencies and cannot replace them as causes.

By its very nature operant behavior encourages the invention of mental or cognitive processes said to initiate action. In a reflex, conditioned or unconditioned, there is a conspicuous prior cause. Something triggers the response. But behavior that has been positively reinforced occurs upon occasions which, though predisposing, are never compelling. The behavior seems to start up suddenly, without advance notice, as if spontaneously generated. Hence the invention of such cognitive entities as intention, purpose, or will. The same issues were debated with respect to the theory of evolution and for the same reason: selection is a special causal mode not easily observed. Because controlling circumstances which lie in an organism's history of reinforcement are obscure, the mental surrogate gets its chance. Under positive reinforcement we do, as we say, what we are free to do; hence the notion of free will as an initiating condition. (I think it was Jonathan Edwards who said that we believe in free will because we know about our behavior but not about its causes.)

When we do not know why people do one thing rather than another, we say that they "choose" or "make decisions." Choosing originally meant examining, scrutinizing, or testing. Etymologically, deciding means cutting off other possibilities, moving in a direction from which there is no return. Choosing and deciding are thus conspicuous forms of behavior, but cognitive psychologists have nevertheless invented internal surrogates. Anatole Rapaport [3] puts it this way: "A subject in a psychological experiment is offered a choice among alternatives and selects one alternative over others." When this happens, he says, "common sense suggests that he is guided by a preference." Common sense does indeed suggest it, and so do cognitive psychologists, but where and what is a preference? Is it anything more than a tendency to do one thing rather than another? When we cannot tell whence the wind cometh and whither it goeth, we say that it "bloweth where it listeth," and common sense, if not cognitive psychology, thus credits it with a preference. (List, by the way, is an example of a term with a physical referent used to refer to a mental process. It means, of course, to lean—as in the list of a ship. And since things usually fall in the direction in which they are leaning, we say that people lean toward a candidate in an election as a rough way of predicting how they will vote. The same metaphor is found in "inclination"; we are "inclined" to vote for X. But it does not follow that we have internal leanings and inclinations which affect our behavior.)

"Intention" is a rather similar term which once meant stretching. The cognitive version is a critical issue in current linguistics. Must the intention of the speaker be taken into account? In an operant analysis verbal behavior is determined by the consequences which follow in a given verbal environment, and consequences are what cognitive psychologists are really talking about when they speak of intentions. All operant behavior "stretches toward" a future even though the only consequences responsible for its strength have already occurred. I go to a drinking fountain "with the intention of getting a drink of water" in the sense that I go because in the past I have got a drink when I have done so. (I may go for the first time, following directions, but that is not an exception; it is an example of rule-governed behavior, of which more later.)

So much for the cognitive internalization of contingencies of reinforcement and the invention of cognitive causes of behavior.

[3] Rapaport, A. *Experimental games and their uses in psychology.* General Learning Press, 1973.

Far more damaging to an effective analysis is the internalization of the environment. The Greeks invented the mind to explain how the real world could be known. For them, to know meant to be acquainted with, to be intimate with. The term cognition itself is related to coitus, as in the biblical sense in which a man is said to know a woman. Having no adequate physics of light and sound nor any chemistry of taste and odor, the Greeks could not understand how a world outside the body, possibly some distance away, could be known. There must be internal copies. Hence cognitive surrogates of the real world.

The distinction between reality and conscious experience has been made so often that it now seems self-evident. Fred Attneave [4] has recently written that "the statement that the world as we know it is a representation is, I think, a truism—there is really no way in which it can be wrong." But there are at least two ways, depending upon the meaning. If the statement means that we can know only representations of the outside world, it is a "truism" only if we are not our bodies but inhabitants located somewhere inside. Our bodies are in contact with the *real* world and can respond to it directly, but if we are tucked away up in the head, we must be content with representations.

Another possible meaning is that knowing is the very process of constructing mental copies of real things, but if that is the case how do we know the copies? Do we make copies of *them?* And is that regress infinite?

Some cognitive psychologists recognize that knowing is action but try to make the point by appealing to another mental surrogate. Knowledge is said to be "a system of propositions." According to one writer, "when we use the word 'see' we refer to a bridge between a pattern of sensory stimulation and knowledge which is propositional." But "propositional" is simply a laundered version of "behavioral," and the "bridge" is between stimuli and behavior and was built when the stimuli were part of the contingencies.

Representational theories of knowledge are modeled on practical behavior. We do make copies of things. We construct representational works of art, because looking at them is reinforced in

4 Attneave, F., *American Psychologist,* July 1974.

much the same way as looking at what they represent. We make maps, because our behavior in following them is reinforced when we arrive at our destination in the mapped territory. But are there internal surrogates? When we daydream, do we first construct copies of reinforcing episodes which we then watch, or do we simply see things once again? And when we learn to get about in a given territory, do we construct cognitive maps which we then follow or do we follow the territory? If we follow a cognitive map, must we learn to do so, and will that require a map of the map? There is no evidence of the mental construction of images to be looked at or maps to be followed. The body responds to the world, at the point of contact; making copies would be a waste of time.

Knowledge is a key term in cognitive theory, and it covers a good deal of ground. It is often contrasted with perception. We are said to be able to *see* that there are three dots on a card but only to *know* that there are thirteen after counting them, even though counting is a form of behavior. After noting that one spiral can be seen to be continuous but that another can be discovered to be so only by tracing, Bela Julesz [5] has said that "any visual task that cannot be performed spontaneously, without effort or deliberation, can be regarded as a cognitive task rather than as a perceptual one," though all the steps in that example are also clearly behavioral.

"Knowing how to do something" is an internal surrogate of behavior in its relation to contingencies. A child learns to ride a bicycle and is then said to possess knowledge of how to ride. The child's behavior has been changed by the contingencies of reinforcement maintained by bicycles; the child has not taken possession of the contingencies.

To speak of knowing *about* things is also to construct an internal surrogate of contingencies. We watch a football game and are then said to possess knowledge of what happened. We read a book and are said to know what it is about. The game and the book are somehow "represented" in our minds: we are "in possession of certain facts." But the evidence is simply that we can describe

[5] Julesz, B., *Scientific American*, April 1975.

what happened at the game and report what the book was about. Our behavior has been changed, but there is no evidence that we have acquired knowledge. To be "in possession of the facts" is not to contain the facts within ourselves but to have been affected by them.

Possession of knowledge implies storage, a field in which cognitive psychologists have constructed a great many mental surrogates of behavior. The organism is said to take in and store the environment, possibly in some processed form. Let us suppose that a young girl saw a picture yesterday and when asked to describe it today, does so. What has happened? A traditional answer would run something like this: when she saw the picture yesterday the girl formed a copy in her mind (which, in fact, was really all she saw). She encoded it in a suitable form and stored it in her memory, where it remained until today. When asked to describe the picture today, she searched her memory, retrieved the encoded copy, and converted it into something like the original picture, which she then looked at and described. The account is modeled on the physical storage of memoranda. We make copies and other records, and respond to them. But do we do anything of the sort in our minds?

If anything is "stored," it is behavior. We speak of the "acquisition" of behavior, but in what form is it possessed? Where is behavior when an organism is not behaving? Where at the present moment, and in what form, is the behavior I exhibit when I am listening to music, eating my dinner, talking with a friend, taking an early morning walk, or scratching an itch? A cognitive psychologist has said that verbal behavior is stored as "lexical memories." Verbal behavior often leaves public records which can be stored in files and libraries, and the metaphor of storage is therefore particularly plausible. But is the expression any more helpful than saying that my behavior in eating my dinner is stored as prandial memories, or scratching an itch as a prurient memory? The observed facts are simple enough: I have acquired a repertoire of behavior, parts of which I display upon appropriate occasions. The metaphor of storage and retrieval goes well beyond those facts.

The computer, together with information theory as designed to deal with physical systems, has made the metaphor of input-storage-retrieval-output fashionable. The struggle to make machines that think like people has had the effect of supporting theories in which people think like machines. Mind has recently been defined as "the system of organizations and structures ascribed to an individual that processess inputs . . . and provides output to the various subsystems and the world." But organizations and structures of what? (The metaphor gains power from the way in which it disposes of troublesome problems. By speaking of input one can forget all the travail of sensory-psychology and physiology; by speaking of output one can forget all the problems of reporting and analyzing action; and by speaking of the storage and retrieval of information one can avoid all the difficult problems of how organisms are indeed changed by contact with their environments and how those changes survive.)

Sensory data are often said to be stored as images, much like the images said to represent the real world. Once inside, they are moved about for cognitive purposes. There is a familiar experiment on color generalization in which a pigeon pecks at a disk of, say, green light, the behavior being reinforced on a variable interval schedule. When a stable rate of responding develops, no further reinforcements are given, and the color of the disk is changed. The pigeon responds to another color at a rate which depends upon how much it differs from the original; rather similar colors evoke fairly high rates, very different colors low rates. A cognitive psychologist might explain the matter in this way: The pigeon takes in a new color (as "input"), retrieves the original color from memory, where it has been stored in some processed form, puts the two colored images side by side so that they may be easily compared, and after evaluating the difference, responds at the appropriate rate. But what advantage is gained by moving from a pigeon that responds to different colors on a disk to an inner pigeon that responds to colored images in its mind? The simple fact is that because of a known history of reinforcement, different colors control different rates.

The cognitive metaphor is based upon behavior in the real world. We store samples of material and retrieve and compare them with other samples. We compare them in the literal sense of putting them side by side to make differences more obvious. And we respond to different things in different ways. But that is all. The whole field of the processing of information can be reformulated as changes in the control exerted by stimuli.

The storage of practical knowledge raises another problem. When I learn, say, to take apart the rings of a puzzle, it seems unlikely that I store my knowledge of how to do so as a copy of the puzzle or of the contingencies the puzzle maintains for those trying to solve it. Instead cognitive theory holds that I store a rule. Rules are widely used as mental surrogates of behavior, in part because they can be memorized and hence "possessed," but there is an important difference between rules and the contingencies they describe. Rules can be internalized in the sense that we can say them to ourselves, but in doing so we do not internalize the contingencies.

I may learn to solve the puzzle in either of two ways. I may move the rings about until I hit upon a response that separates them. The behavior will be strengthened, and if I do the same thing a number of times, I will eventually be able to take the rings apart quickly. My behavior has been shaped and maintained by its effects on the rings. I may, on the other hand, simply follow printed directions supplied with the puzzle. The directions describe behavior that separates the rings, and if I have already learned to follow directions, I can avoid the possibly long process of having my behavior shaped by the contingencies.

Directions are rules. Like advice, warnings, maxims, proverbs, and governmental and scientific laws, they are extremely important parts of a culture, enabling people to profit from the experience of others. Those who have acquired behavior through exposure to contingencies describe the contingencies, and others then circumvent exposure by behaving in the ways described. But cognitive psychologists contend that something of the same sort happens internally when people learn directly from the contingencies. They are said to discover rules which they themselves then follow. But rules are not *in* the contingencies, nor must they be "known" by those who acquire behavior under exposure to them. (We are lucky that this should be so, since rules are verbal products which arose very late in the evolution of the species.)

The distinction between rules and contingencies is currently important in the field of verbal behavior. Children learn to speak through contact with verbal communities, possibly without instruction. Some verbal responses are effective and others not, and over a period of time more and more effective behavior is shaped and maintained. The contingencies having this effect can be analyzed. A verbal *response* "means" something in the sense that the speaker is under the control of particular circumstances; a verbal *stimulus* "means" something in the sense that the listener responds to it in particular ways. The verbal community maintains contingencies of such a nature that responses made upon particular occasions serve as useful stimuli to listeners who then behave appropriately to the occasions.

More complex relations among the behaviors of speaker and listener fall within the fields of syntax and grammar. Until the time of the Greeks, no one seems to have known that there were rules of grammar, although people spoke grammatically in the sense that they behaved effectively under the contingencies maintained by verbal communities, as children today learn to talk without being given rules to follow. But cognitive psychologists insist that speakers and listeners must discover rules for themselves. One authority, indeed, has defined speaking as "engaging in a rule-governed form of intentional behavior." But there is no evidence that rules play any part in the behavior of the ordinary speaker. By using a dictionary and a grammar we may compose acceptable sentences in a language we do not otherwise speak, and we may occasionally consult a dictionary or a grammar in speaking our own language, but even so we seldom speak by applying rules. We speak because our behavior is shaped and maintained by the practices of a verbal community.

Having moved the environment inside the head in the form of conscious experience and behavior in the form of intention, will, and choice, and having stored the effects of contingencies of reinforcement as knowledge and rules, cognitive psychologists put them all together to compose an internal simulacrum of the organism, a kind of doppelgänger, not unlike the classical homunculus, whose behavior is the subject of what Piaget and others have called "subjective behaviorism." The mental apparatus studied by cognitive psychology is simply a rather crude version of contingencies of reinforcement and their effects.

Every so-called cognitive process has a physical model. We *associate* things by putting them together. We *store* memoranda and retrieve them for later use. We *compare* things by putting them side by side to emphasize differences. We *discriminate* things one from another by separating them and treating them in different ways. We *identify* objects by isolating them from confusing surroundings. We *abstract* sets of items from complex arrays. We describe contingencies of reinforcement in *rules*. These are the actions of real persons. It is only in the fanciful world of an inner person that they become mental processes.

The very speed with which cognitive processes are invented to explain behavior should arouse our suspicions. Molière made a joke of a medical example more than three hundred years ago: "I am asked by the learned doctors for the cause and reason why opium puts one to sleep, to which I reply that there is in it a soporific virtue the nature of which is to lull the senses." Molière's candidate could have cited evidence from introspection, invoking a collateral effect of the drug, by saying: "To which I reply that opium makes one feel sleepy." But the soporific virtue itself is a sheer invention, and it is not without current parallels.

A conference was recently held in Europe on the subject of scientific creativity. A report published in *Science* [6] begins by pointing out that more than ninety percent of scientific innovation has been accomplished by fewer than ten percent of all scientists. The next sentence might be paraphrased in this way: "I am asked by the learned doctors for the cause and reason why this should be so, to which I reply that it is because only a few scientists possess creativity." Similarly, "I am asked by the learned doctors for the cause and reason why children learn to talk with great speed, to which I reply that it is because they possess linguistic competence." Molière's audiences laughed.

Cognitive psychologists have two answers to the charge that the mental apparatus is a metaphor or construct. One is that cogni-

_____

[6] *Science*, June 21, 1974.

tive processes are known through introspection. Do not all thinking persons know that they think? And if behaviorists say they do not, are they not either confessing a low order of mentality or acting in bad faith for the sake of their position? No one doubts that behavior involves internal processes; the question is how well they can be known through introspection. As I have argued elsewhere, self-knowledge, consciousness, or awareness became possible only when the species acquired verbal behavior, and that was very late in its history. The only nervous systems then available had evolved for other purposes and did not make contact with the more important physiological activities. Those who see themselves thinking see little more than their perceptual and motor behavior, overt and covert. They could be said to observe the results of "cognitive processes" but not the processes themselves—a "stream of consciousness" but not what causes the streaming, the "image of a lemon" but not the act of associating appearance with flavor, their use of an abstract term but not the process of abstraction, a name recalled but not its retrieval from memory, and so on. We do not, through introspection, observe the physiological processes through which behavior is shaped and maintained by contingencies of reinforcement.

But physiologists observe them and cognitive psychologists point to resemblances which suggest that they and the physiologists are talking about the same things. The very fact that cognitive processes are going on inside the organism suggests that the cognitive account is closer to physiology than the contingencies of reinforcement studied by those who analyze behavior. But if cognitive processes are simply modeled upon the environmental contingencies, the fact that they are assigned to space inside the skin does not bring them closer to a physiological account. On the contrary, the fascination with an imagined inner life has led to a neglect of the observed facts. The cognitive constructs give physiologists a misleading account of what they will find inside.

In summary, then, I am not a cognitive psychologist for several reasons. I see no evidence of an inner world of mental life relative either to an analysis of behavior as a function of environmental forces or to the physiology of the nervous system. The respective sciences of behavior and physiology will move forward most rapidly if their domains are correctly defined and analyzed.

I am equally concerned with practical consequences. The appeal to cognitive states and processes is a diversion which could well be responsible for much of our failure to solve our problems. We need to change our behavior and we can do so only by changing our physical and social environments. We choose the wrong path at the very start when we suppose that our goal is to change the "minds and hearts of men and women" rather than the world in which they live.

9

The Experimental Analysis
of Behavior (A History)

I was drawn to psychology and particularly to behaviorism by some papers which Bertrand Russell published in the *Dial* in the 1920's and which led me to his book *Philosophy* [1] (called in England *An Outline of Philosophy*), the first section of which contains a much more sophisticated discussion of several epistemological issues raised by behaviorism than anything of John B. Watson's. Naturally I turned to Watson himself, but at the time only to his popular *Behaviorism*. [2] I bought Pavlov's *Conditioned Reflexes* [3] shortly after it appeared, and when I came to Harvard for graduate study in psychology I took a course which covered not only conditioned reflexes but the postural and locomotor reflexes of Magnus and the spinal reflexes reported in Sherrington's *Integrative Action of the Nervous System*. [4] The course was taught by Hudson Hoagland in the Department of General Physiology, the head of which,

[1] Russell, B. *Philosophy*. New York: W. W. Norton, 1927.

[2] Watson, J. B. *Behaviorism*. New York: W. W. Norton, 1924.

[3] Pavlov, I. P. *Conditioned reflexes*. Oxford University Press, 1927.

[4] Sherrington, C. S. *Integrative action of the nervous system*. New Haven: Yale University Press, 1906.

W. J. Crozier, had worked with Jacques Loeb and was studying tropisms. I continued to prefer the reflex to the tropism, but I accepted Loeb's and Crozier's dedication to the organism as a whole and the latter's contempt for medical school "organ physiology." Nevertheless, in the Department of Physiology at the Medical School I later worked with Hallowell Davis and with Alexander Forbes, who had been in England with Adrian and was using Sherrington's torsion-wire myograph to study the reflex control of movement.

By the end of my first year at Harvard I was analyzing the behavior of an "organism as a whole" under soundproofed conditions like those described by Pavlov. In one experiment I quietly released a rat into a small dark tunnel from which it could emerge into a well-lighted space, and with moving pen on a moving strip of paper I recorded its exploratory progress, as well as its retreat into the tunnel when I made a slight noise. Some of my rats had babies, and in their early squirmings I thought I saw some of the postural reflexes stereoscopically illustrated in Magnus's *Körperstellung*,[5] and I began to study them. I mounted a light platform on tight wires and amplified its forward-and-backward movement with an arm writing on a smoked drum. I could put a small rat on the platform and record the tremor of its leg muscles when I pulled it gently by the tail, as well as the sudden forward leap with which it often reacted to this stimulation.

I decided to do something of the sort with an adult rat. I built a very light runway about eight feet long, the lengthwise vibration of which I could also amplify and record on a smoked drum, and I induced a rat to run along it by giving it food at the end. When it was halfway along, I would make a slight noise and record the way in which it came to a sudden stop by the effect on the runway. I planned to watch changes as the rat adapted to the noise; possibly I could condition another stimulus to elicit the same response. My records looked a little like those made by a torsion-wire myograph, but they reported the behavior of the organism as a whole.

This was all pretty much in the tradition of reflex physiology, but quite by accident something happened which dramatically

[5] Magnus, R. *Körperstellung.* Berlin: Springer, 1924.

changed the direction of my research. In my apparatus the rat went down a back alley to the other end of the apparatus before making its recorded run, and I noticed that it did not immediately start to do so after being fed. I began to time the delays and found that they changed in an orderly way. Here was a *process,* something like the processes of conditioning and extinction in Pavlov's work, where the details of the act of running, like those of salivation, were not the most important thing.

I have described elsewhere [6] the series of steps through which I simplified my apparatus until the rat simply pushed open the door of a small bin to get a piece of food. Under controlled conditions and with pellets of food which took some time to chew, I found that the rate of eating was a function of the quantity of food already eaten. The title of my first experimental paper, "On the Conditions of Elicitation of Certain Eating Reflexes," [7] shows that I was still applying the concept of the reflex to the behavior of the organism as a whole.

Pushing open a door was conditioned behavior, but in order to study the process of conditioning, 1 needed a more clearly defined act. I chose pushing down a horizontal bar mounted as a lever. When the rat pressed the lever, a pellet of food was released into a tray. The arrangement was, of course, close to that with which Thorndike had demonstrated his Law of Effect, and in my first paper I called my apparatus a "problem box," but the results were quite different. Thorndike's cat learned by dropping out unsuccessful bits of behavior until little or nothing remained but the successful response. Nothing of the sort happened in my experiment. Pavlov's emphasis on the control of conditions had led me to take certain steps to avoid disturbing my rat. I gave it plenty of time to recover from being put into the apparatus by enclosing it first in a special compartment from which I later quietly released it. I left it in the apparatus a long time so that it could become thoroughly accustomed to being there, and I repeatedly operated the food dispenser until the rat was no longer disturbed by the noise and ate

[6] Skinner, B. F. A case history in scientific method. *American Psychologist,* 1956, *11,* 221–233.

[7] Skinner, B. F. On the conditions of elicitation of certain eating reflexes. *Proceedings of the National Academy of Sciences,* 1930, *16,* 433–438.

as soon as food appeared. All this was done when the lever was resting in its lowest position and hence before pressing it could be conditioned. The effect was to remove all the unsuccessful behavior which had composed the learning process in Thorndike's experiment. Many of my rats began to respond at a high rate as soon as they had depressed the lever and obtained only one piece of food.

Conditioning was certainly not the mere survival of a successful response; it was an increase in rate of responding, or in what I called reflex strength. Thorndike had said that the cat's successful behavior was "stamped in," but his evidence was an increasing priority over other behavior which was being "stamped out." The difference in interpretation became clearer when I disconnected the food dispenser and found that the behavior underwent extinction. As R. S. Woodworth [8] later pointed out, Thorndike never investigated the extinction of problem-box behavior.

Though rate of responding was not one of Sherrington's measures of reflex strength, it emerged as the most important one in my experiment. Its significance was clarified by the fact that I recorded the rat's behavior in a cumulative curve; one could read the rate directly as the slope of the curve and see at a glance how it changed over a considerable period of time. Rate proved to be a particularly useful measure when I turned from the acquisition of behavior to its maintenance, in the study of schedules of intermittent reinforcement. Theoretically, it was important because it was relevant to the central question: what is the probability that an organism will engage in a particular form of behavior at a particular time?

I was nevertheless slow in appreciating the importance of the concept of strength of response. For example, I did not immediately shift from "condition" to "reinforce," although the latter term emphasizes the strengthening of behavior. I did not use "reinforce" at all in my first report of the arrangement of lever and food dispenser, and my first designation for intermittent reinforcement was "periodic reconditioning."

Strength or probability of response fitted comfortably into

[8] Woodworth, R. S. *Contemporary schools of psychology.* New York: Ronald Press, 1951.

the formulation of a science of behavior proposed in my thesis. Russell was again responsible for a central point. Somewhere he had said that "reflex" in psychology had the same status as "force" in physics. I knew what that meant because I had read Ernst Mach's *Science of Mechanics*,[9] the works of Henri Poincaré on scientific method, and Bridgman's *Logic of Modern Physics*.[10] My thesis was an operational analysis of the reflex. I insisted that the word should be defined simply as an observed correlation of stimulus and response. Sherrington's synapse was a mere inference which could not be used to explain the facts from which it was inferred. Thus, a stimulus might grow less and less effective as a response was repeatedly elicited, but it did not explain anything to attribute this to "reflex fatigue." Eventually the physiologist would discover a change in the nervous system, but so far as the behavioral facts were concerned, the only identifiable explanation was the repeated elicitation. In my thesis [11] I asserted that in the intact organism "conditioning, 'emotion,' and 'drive' so far as they concern behavior were essentially to be regarded as changes in reflex strength," and I offered my experiments on "drive" and conditioning as examples.

One needed to refer not only to a stimulus and a response but to conditions which changed the relation between them. I called these conditions "third variables," and represented matters with a simple equation:

$$R = f (S, A)$$

where A represented any condition affecting reflex strength, such as the deprivation with which I identified "drive" in the experimental part of my thesis.

The summer after I got my degree, Edward C. Tolman was

[9] Mach, E. *The science of mechanics*. Chicago: Open Court, 1893.

[10] Bridgman, P. W. *The logic of modern physics*. New York: Macmillan, 1928.

[11] Skinner, B. F. The concept of the reflex in the description of behavior. Thesis. Harvard University Library, Cambridge, Massachusetts. (Part One reprinted in B. F. Skinner, *Cumulative record* [3rd ed.]. New York: Appleton-Century-Crofts, 1972, along with 47 other papers.)

teaching at Harvard, and I saw a great deal of him. I expounded my operational position at length and the relevance of third variables in determining reflex strength. Tolman's book *Purposive Behavior in Animals and Men* [12] was then in press, and in it he speaks of "independent variables" but only as such things as genetic endowment or an initiating physiological state. Three years later he published a paper [13] containing the equation:

$$B = f (S, H, T, P)$$

in which B stood for behavior, as my R stood for response, S for "the environmental stimulus setup" (my S), H for heredity, T for "specific past training" (my "conditioning"), and P for "a releasing internal condition of appetite or aversion" (my "drive"). Woodworth later pointed out that these equations were similar. There was, however, an important difference: what I had called a "third variable" Tolman called "intervening." For me the observable operations in conditioning, drive, and emotion lay *outside* the organism, but Tolman put them inside, as replacements for, if not simply redefinitions of, mental processes, and that is where they still are in cognitive psychology today. Ironically, the arrangement is much closer than mine to the traditional reflex arc.

Although rate of responding, in the absence of identifiable stimulation, had no parallel in Sherrington or Pavlov, I continued to talk about reflexes. I assumed that some features of the lever were functioning as stimuli which elicited the response of pressing the lever. But I was unhappy about this, and I began to look more closely at the role of the stimulus. I reinforced pressing the lever when a light was on but not when it was off and found that in the dark the behavior underwent extinction. Turning on the light then appeared to elicit the response, but the history behind that effect could not be ignored. The light was not *eliciting* the behavior; it was functioning as a variable affecting its rate, and it derived its power to do so from the differential reinforcement with which it had been correlated.

[12] Tolman, E. C. *Purposive behavior in animals and men.* New York: Century, 1932.
[13] Tolman, E. C. Philosophy versus immediate experience. *Philosophy of Science,* 1935, 2, 356–380.

In the summer of 1934 I submitted two papers for publication in separate efforts to revise the concept of the reflex. In "The Generic Nature of Stimulus and Response" [14] I argued that neither a stimulus nor a response could be isolated by surgical or other means and that the best clue to a useful unit was the orderliness of the changes in its strength as a function of "third variables." In "Two types of conditioned Reflex and a Pseudo-type" [15] I distinguished between Pavlovian and what I would later call operant conditioning. Quite apart from any internal process, a clear difference could be pointed out in the contingent relations among stimuli, responses, and reinforcement.

I was forced to look more closely at the role of the stimulus when Konorski and Miller [16] replied to the latter paper by describing an experiment they had performed in the late twenties which they felt anticipated my own. They had shocked the paw of a dog and given it food when it flexed its leg. Eventually the leg flexed even though the paw was not shocked. I replied that true reflexes seldom have the kinds of consequences which lead to operant conditioning. Shock may be one way of inducing a hungry dog to flex its leg so that the response can be reinforced with food, but it is an unusual one, and an eliciting stimulus can in fact seldom be identified. (As to priority, Thorndike was, of course, ahead of us all by more than a quarter of a century.)

In my reply [17] I used the term "operant" for the first time and applied "respondent" to the Pavlovian case. It would have been the right time to abandon "reflex," but I was still strongly under the control of Sherrington, Magnus, and Pavlov, and I continued to hold to the term doggedly when I wrote *The Behavior of Organisms* (1938).[18] It took me several years to break free of my own stimulus control in the field of operant behavior. From this point

[14] Skinner, B. F. The generic nature of the concepts of stimulus and response. *Journal of General Psychology*, 1935, *12*, 40–65.

[15] Skinner, B. F. Two types of conditioned reflex and a pseudo type. *Journal of General Psychology*, 1935, *12*, 66–77.

[16] Konorski, J. and Miller, S. On two types of conditioned reflex. *Journal of General Psychology*, 1937, *16*, 264–272.

[17] Skinner, B. F. Two types of conditioned reflex: A reply to Konorski and Miller. *Journal of General Psychology*, 1937, *16*, 272–279.

[18] Skinner, B. F. *The behavior of organisms.* New York: Appleton-Century, 1938.

on, however, I was clearly no longer a stimulus-response psychologist.

The lack of an identifiable eliciting stimulus in operant behavior raises a practical problem: we must wait for behavior to appear before we can reinforce it. We thus start with much less control than in respondent conditioning. Moreover, there is a great deal of complex behavior for which we shall certainly wait in vain, since it will never occur spontaneously. In human behavior there are many ways of "priming" an operant response (that is, evoking it for the first time in order to reinforce it), and one of them is also available in lower organisms: complex behavior can be "shaped" through a series of successive approximations. To reinforce pressing a lever with great force, for example, we cannot simply wait for a very forceful response, but we can differentially reinforce the more forceful of the responses which do occur, with the result that the mean force increases.

I used a similar programming of contingencies of reinforcement to shape complex topography in a demonstration (reported in the *Behavior of Organisms*) in which a rat pulled a chain to release a marble, picked up the marble, carried it across the cage, and dropped it into a tube. The terminal behavior was shaped by a succession of slight changes in the apparatus. Later my colleagues and I discovered that we could avoid the time-consuming process of altering the apparatus by constructing programmed contingencies while reinforcing directly by hand.

I soon tried the procedure on a human subject—our nine-month-old daughter. I was holding her on my lap one evening when I turned on a table lamp beside the chair. She looked up and smiled, and I decided to see whether I could use the light as a reinforcer. I waited for a slight movement of her left hand and turned on the light for a moment. Almost immediately she moved her hand again, and again I reinforced. I began to wait for bigger movements, and within a short time she was lifting her arm in a wide arc—"to turn on the light."

I was writing *Walden Two* [19] at the time, and the book is often cited as an essay in behavioral engineering, but I believe it contains no example of the explicit use of a contrived reinforcer.

[19] Skinner, B. F. *Walden Two*. New York: Macmillan, 1948.

The community functions through positive reinforcement, but the contingencies are in the natural and social environments. They have been carefully designed, but there is no continuing intervention by a reinforcing agent. The only contrived contingencies are Pavlovian: children are "desensitized" to frustration and other destructive emotions by being exposed to situations of carefully graded intensity.

I began to analyze the contingencies of reinforcement to be found in existing cultures in an undergraduate course at Harvard in the spring of 1949. *Science and Human Behavior* (1953) [20] was written as a text for that course, and in it I considered practices in such fields as government, religion, economics, education, psychotherapy, self-control, and social behavior—and all from an operant point of view.

Practical demonstrations soon followed. A graduate student at Indiana, Paul Fuller, had reinforced arm-raising in a twenty-year-old human organism which had never before "shown any sign of intelligence," and in 1953 I set up a small laboratory to study operant behavior in a few backward patients in a mental hospital. Ogden R. Lindsley took over that project and found that psychotics could be brought under the control of contingencies of reinforcement if the contingencies were clear-cut and carefully programmed. Ayllon, Azrin, and many others subsequently used operant conditioning in both management and therapy to improve the lives of psychotic and retarded people.

At the University of Pittsburgh in the spring of 1954 I gave a paper called "The Science of Learning and the Art of Teaching" [21] and demonstrated a machine designed to teach arithmetic, using an instructional program. A year or two later I designed the teaching machines which were used in my undergraduate course at Harvard, and my colleague, James G. Holland, and I wrote the programmed materials eventually published as *The Analysis of Behavior* (1961).[22] The subsequent history of programmed instruction and, on a

[20] Skinner, B. F. *Science and human behavior.* New York: Macmillan, 1953.

[21] Skinner, B. F. The science of learning and the art of teaching. *Harvard Educational Review,* 1954, *24,* 86–97.

[22] Holland, J. G. and Skinner, B. F. *The analysis of behavior.* New York: McGraw-Hill, 1961.

broader scale, of what has come to be called applied behavior analysis or behavior modification is too well known to need further review here.

Meanwhile, the experimental analysis of operant behavior was expanding rapidly as many new laboratories were set up. Charles B. Ferster and I enjoyed a very profitable five-year collaboration. Many of our experiments were designed to discover whether the performance characteristic of a schedule could be explained by the conditions prevailing at the moment of reinforcement, including the recent history of responding, but administrative exigencies drew our collaboration to a close before we had reached a sound formulation, and we settled for the publication of a kind of atlas showing characteristic performances under a wide range of schedules (*Schedules of Reinforcement* [23]). The subsequent development of the field can be traced in the *Journal of the Experimental Analysis of Behavior,* which was founded in 1958.

Several special themes have threaded their way through this history, and some of them call for comment.

Verbal Behavior. I began to explore the subject in the middle thirties. The greater part of a manuscript was written with the help of a Guggenheim Fellowship in 1944–45, from which the William James Lectures at Harvard in 1947 were taken. A sabbatical term in the spring of 1955 enabled me to finish most of a book, which appeared in 1957 as *Verbal Behavior.*[24] It will, I believe, prove to be my most important work. It has not been understood by linguists or psycholinguists, in part because it requires a technical understanding of an operant analysis, but in part because linguists and psycholinguists are primarily concerned with the listener—with what words mean to those who hear them, and with what kinds of sentences are judged grammatical or ungrammatical. The very concept of communication—whether of ideas, meanings, or information—emphasizes transmission to a *listener.* So far as I am concerned, however, very little of the behavior of the listener is worth distinguishing as verbal.

[23] Ferster, C. B. and Skinner, B. F. *Schedules of reinforcement.* New York: Appleton-Century-Crofts, 1957.

[24] Skinner, B. F. *Verbal behavior.* New York: Appleton-Century-Crofts, 1957.

In *Verbal Behavior* verbal operants are classified by reference to the contingencies of reinforcement maintained by a verbal community. The classification is an alternative to the "moods" of the grammarian and the "intentions" of the cognitive psychologist. When these verbal operants come together under multiple causation, the effect may be productive if it contributes, say, to style and wit, but destructive if it leads to distortion and fragmentation. Speakers manipulate their own verbal behavior in order to control or qualify the responses of listeners, and grammar and syntax are "autoclitic" techniques of this sort, as are many other practices in sustained composition. A technology of verbal self-management emerges which is useful both in "discovering what one has to say" and in restricting the range of controlling variables—emphasizing, for example, the kinds of variable (characteristic of logic and science) most likely to lead to effective practical action or the kinds found to be more productive of poetry or fiction.

The Nervous System. My thesis was a sort of declaration of independence from the nervous system, and I restated the position in *The Behavior of Organisms.* It is not, I think, anti-physiological. Various physiological states and processes intervene between the operations performed upon an organism and the resulting behavior. They can be studied with appropriate techniques and there is no question of their importance. A science of behavior has its own facts, however, and they are too often obscured when they are converted into hasty inferences about the nervous system. I would still say, as I said in *The Behavior of Organisms,* that no physiological fact has told us anything about behavior that we did not already know, though we have been told a great deal about the relations between the two fields. The helpful relation is the other way round: a behavioral analysis defines the task of the physiologist. Operant theory and practice now have an important place in the physiological laboratory.

Psychopharmacology. At Minnesota, W. T. Heron and I studied the effects of a few familiar drugs on operant behavior, and in the early fifties, Dr. Peter Dews of the Department of Pharmacology at the Harvard Medical School, became associated with my laboratory and co-workers. At about the same time many of the ethical drug companies set up operant laboratories, some of which contributed to the present armamentarium of behavior-modifying drugs. Operant techniques are now widely used in the field, as well as in the study of drug addiction and related medical problems.

Ethology. Ethologists often assert that their work is neglected by behaviorists, but Watson's first experiments were ethological, and so were mine. The process of operant conditioning itself is part of the genetic equipment of the organism, and I have argued that reinforcers are effective, not because they reduce current drives (a widely held view), but because susceptibilities to reinforcement have had survival value. Species-specific behavior may disrupt operant behavior, but the reverse is also true.

In *Science and Human Behavior* I pointed out that contingencies of survival in natural selection resembled contingencies of reinforcement in operant conditioning. Both involve selection by consequences, a process which, in a work in progress, I argue to be particularly relevant to the question of whether human behavior can indeed take the future into account. Phylogenic contingencies which could have shaped and maintained, say, imitative behavior resemble the contingencies of reinforcement which shape similar behavior in the individual, but one repertoire does not evolve from the other. An experiment on imprinting has shown how an operant analysis may clarify field observations and correct conclusions drawn from them: the young duckling does not inherit the behavior of *following* its mother or an imprinted object; it acquires the behavior because of an innate susceptibility of reinforcement from being close.

A Theory of Knowledge. I came to behaviorism, as I have said, because of its bearing on epistemology, and I have not been disappointed. I am, of course, a radical rather than a methodological behaviorist. I do not believe that there is a world of mentation or subjective experience that is being, or must be ignored. One feels various states and processes within one's body, but these are collateral products of one's genetic and personal histories. No creative or initiating function is to be assigned to them. Introspection does not permit us to make any substantial contribution to physiology, because "we do not have nerves going to the right places." Cognitive psychologists make the mistake of internalizing environmental contingencies—as in speaking of the storage of sensory contacts with the environment in the form of memories which are retrieved and responded to again at some later date. There is a sense in which one *knows* the world, but one does not *possess* knowledge; one behaves because of one's exposure to a complex and subtle genetic and environmental history. As I argued in a final chapter in *Verbal Behavior,* thinking is simply behaving and may be analyzed as such. In *About Behaviorism* [25] I attempted to make a comprehensive statement of the behaviorist's position as I understood it forty-six years after I first entered the field.

Designing a Culture. Walden Two was an early essay in the design of a culture. It was fiction, but I described a supporting science and technology in *Science and Human Behavior.* I was made aware of a basic issue when *Walden Two* was immediately attacked as a threat to freedom. Its protagonist was said to have manipulated the lives of people and to have made an unwarranted use of his own value system. I discussed the issue in a paper called "Freedom and the Control of Men" in 1955 [26] and in a debate with Carl Rogers in 1956.[27] The control of behavior became especially critical with the rise of an applied behavioral analysis in the 1960's, and I returned to the issue in *Beyond Freedom and Dignity* in 1971.[28] Unfortunately that title led many people to believe that I was opposed to freedom and dignity. I did, indeed, argue that people are not in any scientific sense free or responsible for their achievements, but I was concerned with identifying and promoting the conditions under which they *feel* free and worthy. I had no quarrel with the historical struggle to free people from aversive control or from punitive restrictions on the pursuit of happiness, and I proposed that that struggle be continued by shifting to practices which employed positive reinforcement, but I argued that

[25] Skinner, B. F. *About behaviorism.* New York: Alfred A. Knopf, 1974.
[26] Skinner, B. F. Freedom and the control of men. *American Scholar,* Winter 1955–56, *25,* 47–65.
[27] Rogers, C. R. and Skinner, B. F. Some issues concerning the control of human behavior: A symposium. *Science,* 1956, *124,* 1057–1066.
[28] Skinner, B. F. *Beyond freedom and dignity.* New York: Alfred A. Knopf, 1971.

certain aspects of the traditional concepts stood in the way. For example, to make sure that individuals receive credit for their actions, certain punitive practices have actually been perpetuated. I believe that a scientific formulation of human behavior can help us maximize feelings of freedom and dignity.

There is a further goal: what lies beyond freedom and dignity is the survival of the species, and the issues I first discussed in *Walden Two* have become much more pressing as the threat of a catastrophic future becomes clearer. Unfortunately, we move only slowly toward effective action. A question commonly asked is this: when shall we have the behavioral science we need to solve our problems? I believe that the real question is this: when shall we be able to use the behavioral science we already have? More and better science would be helpful, but far more effective decisions would be made in every field of human affairs if those who made them were aware of what we already know.

PART III

EDUCATION

10 *Some Implications of Making Education More Efficient*

11 *The Free and Happy Student*

12 *Designing Higher Education*

10

Some Implications of Making Education More Efficient

There is little doubt that education is in trouble. It faces many different kinds of problems, for which many different kinds of solutions will have to be found. One of them is economic. The educational assignment grows steadily greater. For example, children are to start school at an earlier age, special classes are to be arranged for exceptional children, students are to be admitted to college with fewer qualifications, and new fields are to be covered to improve the relevance of education. These changes come at a time when costs are rising sharply. Tuition and taxes continue to rise, teachers are asked to take on more work and cut down on outside activities, and many schools, particularly parochial schools, are closing.

One solution to the economic problem is simply to make instruction more efficient. If we could teach, say, twice as much in the same time and with the same effort, our present staff and facilities would suffice to teach more students, teach each one more, allow for a wider range of abilities, and cover more fields, while at the same time holding smaller classes, giving teachers a more reasonable workday and more pay, and getting more support from the public by giving more in return for its money. Almost any other enterprise would try to solve an economic problem in that way. It would see whether its practices could not be made more efficient. But teachers and school administrators seldom look in that direction. Why?

Past experience with research in the field of learning may be at fault. The learning curves obtained with mazes and the forgetting curves obtained with memory drums have never given the teacher any real help. Educational psychologists soon turned from basic research on the processes underlying teaching to the measurement of their effects—a change exemplified in the personal history of Edward L. Thorndike.

Part of the explanation may be a distaste for pedagogy or educational method. Can teaching really be taught? Does not any reasonably intelligent person already know what is needed? A teacher must attract the students' attention and keep them interested, but he will have learned how to do this in his daily life. The neglect of pedagogy is seen in current books which tell us how to improve our schools. One needs no special vocabulary or any scientific knowledge to read the contributions of men like John Holt, Jonathan Kozol, Paul Goodman, and Charles Silberman. Even the teaching aids which are most commonly mentioned (audiovisual devices and television, for example) simply do what people do and make no use of a more technical analysis of basic processes. Teaching, in other words, is regarded not as a special skill but as an art in dealing with people. The only problem is to find those who practice it well.

Many educators have gone a step further. They show no interest in making teaching more efficient because they do not believe in teaching. In the classical expression, the teacher cannot teach, he can only help the student learn, and he cannot help much. Carl Rogers has recently said that in his opinion teaching is a "vastly overrated function." [1] "Free schools" (for example, Summerhill) and many experimental colleges boast of how little teaching ac-

---

[1] Rogers, C. *Freedom to learn*. Columbus, Ohio: Merrill, 1969.

tually goes on, and Ivan Illich [2] has completed the reductio ad absurdum by calling for the deschooling of society. It will be enough simply to make the world a "livable learning environment." There is often a note of despair in these proposals. We have tried so hard and failed so miserably; there must be a better way.

The way that is most often suggested goes back to Jean Jacques Rousseau. We are to let the child learn in school as he learns in the world at large—through a natural love of learning, a natural curiosity. Let him know the joy of discovery. The proposal is especially appealing in contrast with what goes on in the joyless punitive schools which have so long characterized education. It is also attractive because it seems to raise no problems. The real world is conveniently at hand and it does not need to be made to work. But Rousseau's proposal has been tried, episodically at least, for two hundred years and that is presumably time enough to demonstrate its feasibility. Why, then, are we still at the stage of making proposals? Why is it that the average life of an experimental free school is said to be something on the order of eighteen months? It is true that new proposals in education, as elsewhere, are not likely to be well supported, and that the great changes which need to be made in established practices can be made only slowly. Nevertheless, more progress should have been made.

A more likely explanation is that the real world is not an effective teacher. Children do not learn much from the natural environment. The feral child, the child said to have been raised by wolves, or one said to have matured alone in a benevolent environment, is about all we have to show for unaided natural curiosity or a love of learning. A physical environment breeds awkward, dangerous, and superstitious behavior, and a social environment breeds hostile as well as friendly behavior, selfish as well as generous behavior. What seem like successful demonstrations of "free" classrooms must be attributed to unanalyzed skills in dealing with people, and the difficulty is that because they have not been analyzed, they cannot be transmitted. There has been no accumulation of better ways of teaching within Rousseau's program. On the contrary, apparent successes have usually meant a contraction in the educational assignment. Less and less is taught, by definition, as learning is left to the natural environment, but to that we must add that less and less is learned. The extent to which we have accepted this consequence is suggested by current proposals to reduce if not abolish "compulsory education."

Education is an important function of a culture—possibly in the long run its most important or only function. A culture, as a social environment, must transmit itself to its new members. Some transmission occurs when new members learn from those with whom they are in contact, with or without informal instruction; but transmission on a scale needed to make people maximally effective needs a carefully designed system.

A lack of confidence in any effort to improve teaching is especially crucial because there are many other reasons why new practices are not likely to be adopted. So far as most administrators and teachers are concerned, an improvement in teaching will demand troublesome changes, in which much is to be lost and not much to be gained. No penalty is imposed if an administrator or teacher overlooks a better way of teaching, and current inefficiencies can be justified by arguing that the task is too difficult, that there are too many students, that facilities are inadequate, and that social and racial problems are insurmountable. If this is not enough, it is possible to fall back upon that argument which has always been used to exonerate bad teaching; it is the student who fails the course, not the teacher or school.

It is a hopeful sign that administrators and teachers are beginning to be held accountable for their work. This has always been true in other professions. A doctor may not cure every patient, but if he cures few or none, he fails as a doctor. A lawyer may not win every case, but if he wins few or none, he will not last long as a lawyer. The salesman may not make every sale, but if he makes few or none, he fails as a salesman. And of course artisans have always been judged in terms of the quality of their work. Why should the teacher not also be held accountable for the results of his teaching?

The commonest answer is that the results cannot be evaluated. They are not as obvious as a cure, a favorable verdict, a sale, or a job well done. Some specialists in educational measurement, in a surprising reversal of an earlier position, have been quick to agree. For more than half a century we have been told that measures of ability and achievement are reliable and valid. But suddenly they have become socially relevant: intelligence has taken on racial overtones, and achievement has been tied to the accountability of teachers. Some authorities are therefore beating a retreat. Henry S. Dyer, vice-president of the Educational Testing Service, has characterized tests of intelligence and of grade equivalency as "monstrosities" and has said that the development of tests which could be used to hold teachers accountable for their work would be an enterprise of the order of magnitude of the atomic bomb.[3] But *students* have been held accountable with the same kinds of tests for decades; they have been admitted to college according to measured abilities and promoted and graduated according to measured achievements. (That we should not hold students accountable, that we should admit them to college regardless of measured abilities and give no examinations to measure their achievement is, of course, part of the philosophy of a natural learning environment.)

It is no doubt easier to measure some effects of teaching than others. How well a student has learned to read is more obvious than what he has learned in, say, social studies. But education would be in serious trouble if we could not tell whether a student has learned anything in social studies. Both the teacher and the student need evidence of progress. One source of trouble is the traditional practice of defining the goals of education in terms of mental processes. If the teacher is to "transmit knowledge," "cultivate skills," "evoke ideas," or "change attitudes," neither he nor the student is likely to have any clear evidence that a change has occurred. Another source of trouble is that the very large repertoire acquired in a course cannot be reliably sampled in a brief examination. We shall see how these problems can be solved in other ways.

Teachers and administrators are likely to reject any proposal that they be held accountable, mainly for economic reasons. There is always the danger that a teacher who is not very efficient will be fired or paid less than one who is conspicuously successful. But only

[3] *New York Times,* March 23, 1971.

when the administrator or teacher is held accountable will he search most actively for better ways of teaching.

It would be unfair to say that teachers and administrators do little to make teaching more effective only because they lack economic incentives. A better explanation is that they do not know what to do. It has always been supposed that the principal source of technical knowledge in education is classroom experience. The young teacher learns how to teach either by teaching or by emulating someone who has learned how to teach by teaching. The possibility that technical help may come from outside the profession is seldom recognized. There was a comparable stage in the history of medicine. Medical practices were once entirely the product of the experience of physicians, but most physicians accept the fact that advances in medicine will now come from the scientific laboratory. A change in provenance is inevitable as soon as a relevant science appears, and that stage has now been reached in education.

What has come to be called the "experimental analysis of behavior" has already given rise to an effective technology of teaching, although it is not yet widely known or used. Three contributions may be noted. One has to do with the teacher's assignment. It has long been supposed that the task of the teacher is to impart *information,* train the *mind,* help the student *grasp relations,* teach him to *appreciate* literature, art and music, encourage *creativity,* and change his *attitudes* (for example, toward racial problems). But the teacher does not act upon the mind or its faculties, or upon traits of character or personality. He acts upon the behavior of the student, and he does so by changing the verbal or nonverbal environment in which the student lives.

It is not always easy to redefine the goals of teaching. In particular, an analysis of the so-called higher mental processes may be quite complex. But progress has already been made, and it has given the teacher a clearer conception of his assignment and better evidence of the extent to which it has been fulfilled. It has also made it less likely that he will seek exoneration for failure by inventing mental objectives which he can claim to have achieved. He is less likely to discount the fact that a child cannot read by arguing that he is acquiring reading readiness or an interest in reading, or that a student who cannot solve problems in arithmetic is nevertheless learning to understand mathematics or acquiring a love for it.

A second contribution of the experimental analysis of behavior has to do with classroom management. Why does a student come to school, behave well in class, pay attention, apply himself to his assignments, answer questions, and so forth? So far as traditional practice is concerned, the answer is simple: to avoid the consequences of not doing so. It is now clear that many of the disciplinary problems faced by teachers (truancy, vandalism, and apathy) are the by-products of a long history of aversive control, which has not yet come to an end. The experimental analysis of behavior has suggested powerful alternatives through the use of positively reinforcing consequences. To put it roughly, the student can be given positive reasons for doing the kinds of things which will advance his education. The layman speaks of these as rewards and may object to new classroom practices as bribery, but to do so is to misunderstand the whole science of contingency management. What is important is not only the rewarding things a student gets but the ways in which they are contingent upon his behavior. The power of contingency management in the classroom is well established—though, again, it is not yet widely used.

The experimental analysis of behavior has made a third contribution to education in the design of instructional materials—both in the material itself and in modes of presentation. Techniques of shaping complex behavior through a program of progressive approximation emerged from the operant laboratory, particularly in the extension of basic principles to the analysis of verbal behavior. The main features of a good program are well known: the student is asked to proceed in small steps and to master each step before moving on to the next. Material is so designed that correct responses are highly probable, and progress through a program may be all that is needed to keep the student at work. A good program imparts an extensive repertoire in a very efficient way.

The personalized system of instruction (PSI) designed by F. S. Keller [4] brings these contributions together in the redesign of courses in colleges and graduate schools. The basic elements have been described by Keller as follows:

> (1) the go-at-your-own-pace feature which permits a student to move through a course of study at a speed commensurate with his ability and other demands upon his time; (2) the unit-perfection requirement for advance, which lets the student go ahead to any material only after demonstrating mastery of that which precedes it; (3) the use of lectures and demonstrations as vehicles of motivation rather than sources of critical information; (4) the related stress upon the written word in teacher communication; and, finally, (5) the use of [a] proctor (student), which permits repeated testing, immediate scoring, almost unavoidable tutoring, and a marked enhancement of his personal social aspect of the educational process (p. 13).

The PSI system is spreading rapidly throughout colleges and universities, and there is no reason why it cannot be adapted to high school and the lower grades.

The definition of objectives in behavioral terms, the design of effective classroom contingencies, and the programming of instructional materials may be all that is needed to solve many current problems in education. Operant conditioning is a matter of both "acquisition" and "motivation," and signs of progress through a program are for most students a highly reinforcing consequence. Individualized treatment removes the greatest source of inefficiency in traditional instruction—the requirement that large numbers of students advance at the same speed, which is almost necessarily the wrong speed for most of them. But perhaps the most important result is that there is no need for final examinations. In a well-designed course of instruction, the behavior a student is acquiring is obvious because he uses it in pursuing the course. A glance ahead shows him what he does not yet know; a glance backward shows him what he

[4] Keller, F. S. Neglected rewards in the educational process. *Proceedings of the Twenty-Third Annual Meeting of the American Conference of Academic Deans.* Los Angeles, 1967. Pp. 9–22.

has learned. Both student and teacher can see what has been done without trying to sample large repertoires. Such instruction is rather like teaching a manual skill or a sport. The golf instructor does not give his student a final examination, measuring the length of ten drives from a tee, the distances from the pin in ten approaches from a sand trap, and scoring the number of successes in ten long putts and ten short putts, and then assign a grade showing how well his student has learned to play. Each step in a program may be considered an examination because the student responds and his response is evaluated. In the Keller system brief tests are taken to determine mastery at each level, but this is very different from trying to measure all that a student has learned at the end of a course.

Impending examinations have well-known emotional effects due, in part, to the feared risk of inaccurate sampling. Administrators and teachers also, faced with accountability, are now beginning to show these effects and for the same reasons. But a well-designed course of instruction solves the problem for both students and teachers. The course itself is the examination. If the student is to receive a grade, it will indicate only how far he has advanced. It is not necessary to determine the degree to which the materials of the whole course are retained, since most of them must have been retained in order to finish the course. The critic may complain that retention is not being measured, but a final examination does not measure it successfully, and it encourages practices, such as last-minute cramming, which actually interfere with the retention the examination is designed to guarantee.

How much improvement is to be expected? Is it fair to say that what is now taught could be taught in half the time and with half the effort on the part of student and teacher? Anyone who has worked through a well-designed program of instruction (in a subject with which he was not until then familiar), anyone who has seen a high school class under good contingency management, or anyone who has talked with or read the reports of students in a personalized system of instruction will be inclined to say yes. Comparisons with so-called control groups in set experiments are not very helpful. The comparison should be with what now prevails in our schools and colleges. There are no doubt other ways in which teaching can be made more effective, but the practices derived from an experimental analysis of behavior already have shown great promise.

We shall not be in the clear, however, until other problems have been solved. Simply to change from a system in which large numbers of students progress at the same rate to a truly individualized mode of instruction may mean drastic changes in the architecture of schools, in the roles of supervisors and teachers, and in daily routines. "More efficient instruction" should mean, if it means anything, that students will learn more rapidly, but if the first-grade teacher also teaches what has been reserved for the second grade, what is the second-grade teacher to teach? The recent history of education in America has been marked by a postponement of instruction—for example, until students are "ready"—but the trend may now be reversed. A classical example is the course in logic designed by Professor Layman Allen of Yale University Law School. The course worked so well with law students that it was tried in college, and it worked so well there that it was tried in high school. At last report it was being taught in the sixth grade. What happens to a standard curriculum when changes of that magnitude become possible?

A reasonable answer might be that students will be taught a great deal more during the same period of instruction. But it may be tempting, instead, to terminate education at an earlier age and this raises other problems. What happens to employment figures if large numbers of young people are turned loose on the job market at an earlier age? (The terminal age in Britain has recently been raised one year, in part, it is said, to solve such a problem.)

Improved instruction will also affect the employment of teachers. Individualized instruction could mean a return to the tutorial practices which existed before there were schools in the present sense, and that may mean that more teachers will be needed. But tutorial instruction was not feasible for large numbers and is clearly out of the reach of present educational systems. Hence the search for new types of materials suitable for self-instruction and for devices which evaluate students' responses to such materials. The Keller system takes advantage of the fact that one learns most effectively when teaching, that individualized instruction may be furthered by letting students teach each other. These solutions seem to suggest that it will eventually be possible to dispense with teachers. But any increase in efficiency brings added educational objectives within reach, many of which demand personal attention.

A loss in personal contact between student and teacher is not necessarily a disadvantage in some fields of learning. The student does not need a person to tell him whether he has correctly translated a particular sentence or solved a problem. The "approval" offered by a teacher differs from the confirmation to be found in programmed materials, but it is not a "natural" consequence of behaving correctly and may, in fact, cause trouble. And before regretting a loss in personal contact, we should look at the kinds which now prevail in classrooms. When large numbers of students are taught at the same time, few of them acquire effective verbal behavior, oral or written. In multiple-choice examinations and in some kinds of programmed materials, students merely check sentences which have been composed by others. They have no chance to learn to compose sentences themselves. Programmed materials can teach effective composition, but the flexibility characteristic of social discourse calls for a teacher as an essential figure because verbal exchange is almost necessarily individualized. We may see a revival of the art of speaking and writing, and it will be important because it involves much of the art of thinking.

Improved efficiency in education makes time available for a greater emphasis on personal exchange between teacher and student. In addition, the teacher remains an essential figure in following the progress of a student and advising him on different courses of action. These new demands will require new kinds of training, and some direct contact with the experimental analysis of behavior may be needed if the teacher is to take advantage of available behavioral technology. The important thing is that more efficient practices will give the teacher far greater power in fulfilling a far more explicit assignment, and that should mean a vast improvement in the status of the teaching profession.

II

The Free
and Happy Student

His name is Emile. He was born in the middle of the eighteenth century in the first flush of the modern concern for personal freedom. His father was Jean-Jacques Rousseau, but he has had many foster parents, among them Pestalozzi, Froebel, and Montessori, down to A. S. Neill and Ivan Illich. He is an ideal student. Full of goodwill toward his teachers and his peers, he needs no discipline. He studies because he is naturally curious. He learns things because they interest him.

Unfortunately, he is imaginary. He was quite explicitly so with Rousseau, who put his own children in an orphanage and preferred to say how he would teach his fictional hero; but the modern version of the free and happy student to be found in books by Paul Goodman, John Holt, Jonathan Kozol, or Charles Silberman is also imaginary. Occasionally a real example seems to turn up. There are teachers who would be successful in dealing with people anywhere —as statesmen, therapists, businessmen, or friends—and there are students who scarcely need to be taught, and together they sometimes seem to bring Emile to life. And unfortunately they do so just often enough to sustain the old dream. But Emile is a will-o'-the-wisp, who has led many teachers into a conception of their role which could prove disastrous.

The student who has been taught *as if he were Emile* is, however, almost too painfully real. It has taken a long time for him to make his appearance. Children were first made free and happy in kindergarten, where there seemed to be no danger in freedom, and for a long time they were found nowhere else, because the rigid discipline of the grade schools blocked progress. But eventually they broke through—moving from kindergarten into grade school, taking over grade after grade, moving into secondary and on into college and, very recently, into graduate school. Step by step they have insisted upon their rights, justifying their demands with the slogans that philosophers of education have supplied. If sitting in rows restricts personal freedom, unscrew the seats. If order can be maintained only through coercion, let chaos reign. If one cannot be really free while worrying about examinations and grades, down with examinations and grades! The whole establishment is now awash with free and happy students.

If they are what Rousseau's Emile would really have been like, we must confess to some disappointment. The Emile we know doesn't work very hard. "Curiosity" is evidently a moderate sort of thing. Hard work is frowned upon because it implies a "work ethic," which has something to do with discipline.

The Emile we know doesn't learn very much. His "interests" are evidently of limited scope. Subjects that do not appeal to him he calls irrelevant. (We should not be surprised at this since Rousseau's Emile, like the boys in Summerhill, never got past the stage of a knowledgeable craftsman.) He may defend himself by questioning the value of knowledge. Knowledge is always in flux, so why bother to acquire any particular stage of it? It will be enough to remain curious and interested. In any case the life of feeling and emotion is to be preferred to the life of intellect; let us be governed by the heart rather than the head.

The Emile we know doesn't think very clearly. He has had little or no chance to learn to think logically or scientifically and is easily taken in by the mystical and the superstitious. Reason is irrelevant to feeling and emotion.

And, alas, the Emile we know doesn't seem particularly happy. He doesn't like his education any more than his predecessors liked theirs. Indeed, he seems to like it less. He is much more inclined to play truant (big cities have given up enforcing truancy laws), and he drops out as soon as he legally can, or a little sooner. If he goes to college, he probably takes a year off at some time in his four-year program. And after that his dissatisfaction takes the form of anti-intellectualism and a refusal to support education.

Are there offsetting advantages? Is the free and happy student less aggressive, kinder, more loving? Certainly not toward the schools and teachers that have set him free, as increasing vandalism and personal attacks on teachers seem to show. Nor is he particularly well disposed toward his peers. He seems perfectly at home in a world of unprecedented domestic violence.

Is he perhaps more creative? Traditional practices were said to suppress individuality; what kind of individuality has now emerged? Free and happy students are certainly different from the students of a generation ago, but they are not very different from each other. Their own culture is a severely regimented one, and their creative works—in art, music, and literature—are confined to primitive and elemental materials. They have very little to be creative with, for they have never taken the trouble to explore the fields in which they are now to be front-runners.

Is the free and happy student at least more effective as a citizen? Is he a better person? The evidence is not very reassuring. Having dropped out of school, he is likely to drop out of life too. It would be unfair to let the hippie culture represent young people today, but it does serve to clarify an extreme. The members of that culture do not accept responsibility for their own lives; they sponge on the contributions of those who have not yet been made free and happy—who have gone to medical school and become doctors, or who have become the farmers who raise the food or the workers who produce the goods they consume.

These are no doubt overstatements. Things are not that bad, nor is education to be blamed for all the trouble. Nevertheless, there is a trend in a well-defined direction, and it is particularly clear in education. Our failure to create a truly free and happy student is symptomatic of a more general problem.

What we may call the struggle for freedom in the Western world can be analyzed as a struggle to escape from or avoid punitive or coercive treatment. It is characteristic of the human species to act in such a way as to reduce or terminate irritating, painful, or dangerous stimuli, and the struggle for freedom has been directed toward those who would control others with stimuli of that sort. Education has had a long and shameful part in the history of that struggle. The Egyptians, Greeks, and Romans all whipped their students. Medieval sculpture showed the carpenter with his hammer and the schoolmaster with the tool of his trade too, and it was the cane or rod. We are not yet in the clear. Corporal punishment is still used in many schools, and there are calls for its return where it has been abandoned.

A system in which students study primarily to avoid the consequences of not studying is neither humane nor very productive. Its by-products include truancy, vandalism, and apathy. Any effort to eliminate punishment in education is certainly commendable. We ourselves act to escape from aversive control, and our students should escape from it too. They should study because they want to, because they like to, because they are interested in what they are doing. The mistake—a classical mistake in the literature of freedom —is to suppose that they will do so as soon as we stop punishing them. Students are not literally free when they have been freed from their teachers. They then simply come under the control of other conditions, and we must look at those conditions and their effects if we are to improve teaching.

Those who have attacked the "servility" of students, as Montessori called it, have often put their faith in the possibility that young people will learn what they need to know from the "world of things," which includes the world of people who are not teachers. Montessori saw possibly useful behavior being suppressed by schoolroom discipline. Could it not be salvaged? And could the environment of the schoolroom not be changed so that other useful behavior would occur? Could the teacher not simply guide the student's natural development? Or could he not accelerate it by teasing out behavior which would occur naturally but not so quickly if he did not help? In other words, could we not bring the real world into the classroom, as John Dewey put it, or destroy the classroom and turn the student over to the real world, as Ivan Illich has recommended. All these possibilities can be presented in an attractive light, but they neglect two vital points:

(*a*) No one learns very much from the real world without help. The only evidence we have of what can be learned from a non-social world has been supplied by those wild boys said to have been raised without contact with other members of their own species. Much more can be learned without formal instruction in a social world, but not without a good deal of teaching, even so. Formal education has made a tremendous difference in the extent of the skills and knowledge which can be acquired by a person in a single lifetime.

(*b*) A much more important principle is that the real world teaches only what is relevant to the present; it makes no explicit preparation for the future. Those who would minimize teaching have contended that no preparation is needed, that the student will follow a natural line of development and move into the future in the normal course of events. We should be content, as Carl Rogers has put it, to trust

> the insatiable curiosity which drives the adolescent boy to absorb everything he can see or hear or read about gasoline engines in order to improve the efficiency and speed of his "hot rod." I am talking about the student who says, "I am discovering, drawing in from the out-side, and making that which is drawn in a real part of me." I am talking about my learning in which the experience of the learner progresses along the line: "No, no, that's not what I want"; "Wait! This is closer to what I'm interested in, what I need." "Ah, here it is! Now I'm grasping and comprehending what I need and what I want to know!" [1]

Rogers is recommending a total commitment to the present moment, or at best to an immediate future.

[1] Rogers, C. *Freedom to learn.* Columbus, Ohio: Merrill, 1969.

But it has always been the task of formal education to set up behavior which would prove useful or enjoyable *later* in the student's life. Punitive methods had at least the merit of providing current reasons for learning things that would be rewarding in the future. We object to the punitive reasons, but we should not forget their function in making the future important.

It is not enough to give the student advice—to explain that he will have a future, and that to enjoy himself and be more successful in it he must acquire certain skills and knowledge now. Mere advice is ineffective because it is not supported by current rewards. The positive consequences that generate a useful behavioral repertoire need not be any more explicitly relevant to the future than were the punitive consequences of the past. The student needs current reasons, positive or negative, but only the educational policy maker who supplies them need take the future into account. It follows that many instructional arrangements seem "contrived," but there is nothing wrong with that. It is the teacher's function to contrive conditions under which students learn. Their relevance to a future usefulness need not be obvious.

It is a difficult assignment. The conditions the teacher arranges must be powerful enough to compete with those under which the student tends to behave in distracting ways. In what has come to be called "contingency management in the classroom" tokens are sometimes used as rewards or reinforcers. They become reinforcing when they are exchanged for reinforcers that are already effective. There is no "natural" relation between what is learned and what is received. The token is simply a reinforcer that can be made clearly contingent upon behavior. To straighten out a wholly disrupted classroom something as obvious as a token economy may be needed, but less conspicuous contingencies—as in a credit-point system, perhaps, or possibly in the long run merely expressions of approval on the part of teacher or peer—may take over.

The teacher can often make the change from punishment to positive reinforcement in a surprisingly simple way—by responding to the student's successes rather than his failures. Teachers have too often supposed that their role is to point out what students are doing wrong, but pointing to what they are doing *right* will often make an enormous difference in the atmosphere of a classroom and in the efficiency of instruction. Programmed materials are helpful in bringing about these changes, because they increase the frequency with which the student enjoys the satisfaction of being right, and they supply a valuable intrinsic reward in providing a clear indication of progress. A good program makes a step in the direction of competence almost as conspicuous as a token.

Programmed instruction is perhaps most successful in attacking punitive methods by allowing the student to move at his own pace. The slow student is released from the punishment which inevitably follows when he is forced to move on to material for which he is not ready, and the fast student escapes the boredom of being forced to go too slow. These principles have recently been extended to college education, with dramatic results, in the Keller system of personalized instruction.[2]

There is little doubt that a student can be given nonpunitive reasons for acquiring behavior that will become useful or otherwise reinforcing at some later date. He can be prepared for the future. But what *is* that future? Who is to say what the student should learn? Those who have sponsored the free and happy student have argued that it is the student himself who should say. His current interests should be the source of an effective educational policy. Certainly they will reflect his idiosyncrasies, and that is good, but how much can he know about the world in which he will eventually play a part? The things he is "naturally" curious about are of current and often temporary interest. How many things must he possess besides his "hot rod" to provide the insatiable curiosity relevant to, say, a course in physics?

It must be admitted that the teacher is not always in a better position. Again and again education has gone out of date as teachers have continued to teach subjects which were no longer relevant at any time in the student's life. Teachers often teach simply what they know. (Much of what is taught in private schools is determined by what the available teachers can teach.) Teachers tend to teach what they can teach easily. Their current interests, like those of students, may not be a reliable guide.

[2] *PSI Newsletter,* October 1972 (published by the Center for Personalized Instruction, Georgetown University).

Nevertheless, in recognizing the mistakes that have been made in the past in specifying what students are to learn, we do not absolve ourselves from the responsibility of setting educational policy. We should say, we should be *willing* to say, what we believe students will need to know, taking the individual student into account wherever possible, but otherwise making our best prediction with respect to students in general. Value judgments of this sort are not as hard to make as is often argued. Suppose we undertake to prepare the student to produce his share of the goods he will consume and the services he will use, to get on well with his fellows, and to enjoy his life. In doing so are we imposing *our* values on someone else? No, we are merely choosing a set of specifications which, so far as we can tell, will at some time in the future prove valuable to the student and his culture. Who is any more likely to be right?

The natural, logical outcome of the struggle for personal freedom in education is that the teacher should improve his control of the student rather than abandon it. The free school is no school at all. Its philosophy signalizes the abdication of the teacher. The teacher who understands his assignment and is familiar with the behavioral processes needed to fulfill it can have students who not only feel free and happy while they are being taught but who will continue to feel free and happy when their formal education comes to an end. They will do so because they will be successful in their work (having acquired useful productive repertoires), because they will get on well with their fellows (having learned to understand themselves and others), because they will enjoy what they do (having acquired the necessary knowledge and skills), and because they will from time to time make an occasional creative contribution toward an even more effective and enjoyable way of life. Possibly the most important consequence is that the teacher will then feel free and happy too.

We must choose today between Cassandran and Utopian prognostications. Are we to work to avoid disaster or to achieve a better world? Again, it is a question of punishment or reward. Must we act because we are frightened, or are there positive reasons for changing our cultural practices? The issue goes far beyond education, but it is one with respect to which education has much to offer. To escape from or avoid disaster, people are likely to turn to the punitive measures of a police state. To work for a better world, they may turn instead to the positive methods of education. When it finds its most effective methods, education will be almost uniquely relevant to the task of setting up and maintaining a better way of life.

12

Designing
Higher Education

*The principal function of education is to transmit the culture
—to enable new members of a group to profit from what others have
already learned. It follows that the principal task of the student is
to learn what others already know.*

These are not popular contentions. They do not seem compatible with a conception of the teacher as one who helps the student discover the world for himself, or who stimulates a natural curiosity, or who guides intellectual, emotional, or moral development, or who makes the learning process more meaningful. On the contrary, teaching as the transmission of what is already known is often openly attacked as imposing the teacher's values on the student, as intervening in a natural process of growth, and as undermining the freedom and dignity of the student. The teacher is enjoined to avoid telling what he knows and to look for meaningful interchanges of other kinds.

If we ask for supporting evidence of the benefits which follow, we are likely to be told that the effects of these alternative practices are not measurable. Measurement is appropriate only to the transmission of what is already known. We must not expect to quantify the extent to which a teacher helps a student discover the world for himself, or arouses his curiosity, or guides his development, or makes learning meaningful. Quantifiable evidence may well indicate that new ways of teaching have been less effective (the student has indeed learned less of what is already known), but he has undergone other, more important, changes, the evidence of which is necessarily qualitative. In fact, examinations mean little and should be abolished.

The qualitative evidence is not always reassuring, however. Practices designed to replace the transmission of what is already known have had some unanticipated effects which can scarcely be said to recommend them. For example—

1. The student who from kindergarten through college has been commended by teachers who are on the alert for signs of discovery is likely to have an exaggerated notion of his powers of discovery and of how much he has actually learned.

2. When tradition is dismissed as restrictive and creative efforts therefore start from scratch, works of art, music, and literature are necessarily, in a quite literal sense, primitive.

3. Those who have been left to learn how to think by themselves are quite unable to discover all the techniques which have accumulated over the centuries. With respect to intellectual self-management, they are therefore almost defenseless against bad logic, superstition, mystical nonsense, and demagoguery. Their ethical self-management is similarly defective. It is not surprising that some of them should have tried to make a virtue of irrationality.

4. Many cultural practices have prevailed because they support behavior which "takes the future into account": they give people current reasons for behaving in ways which have important though possibly remote consequences. Those who confine themselves to matters of current relevance lack this support and are forced to be, in the strictest sense, existentialists; they have not discovered the past and have no reason for behaving effectively with respect to a future.

The picture is not so bleak as I have painted it, because no teacher *merely* aids discovery, or stimulates curiosity, or guides development, or makes learning meaningful. Students do read books, enter into informative discussions, listen to music, see works of art, and thus learn about what others have said and done and how they have said and done it. Some transmission of the culture has gone on, as it were, under the counter. Many contemporary educational philosophers nevertheless seem dedicated to minimizing transmission, and I believe that they have done so for ideological reasons largely unrelated to education.

It is easy to be misled by what I have called the Idols of the School.[1] The Idol of the Good Teacher is the belief that what a good teacher can do any teacher can do, and the Idol of the Good Student is the belief that what a good student can learn any student can learn. For reasons which are still beyond analysis, teachers are sometimes extraordinarily effective even when their students are not outstanding, and students sometimes learn a great deal even without the help of good teachers. A combination of good teacher and good student may have almost miraculous results. Nothing much needs to be done about higher education when these conditions prevail, but we must not forget the vast numbers of ordinary teachers who cannot profit from the selection of good students, or the vast numbers of ordinary students who do not have good teachers. For them, effective educational practices must be designed.

An effective design must be based upon an understanding of behavioral processes. The basic questions are these: Why should anyone teach, and why should anyone learn? They are questions about human behavior, and recent advances in the analysis of behavior are helpful in answering them.

Education was once mainly punitive. The rod, the cane, and the dunce cap were the schoolmaster's tools. The student learned or suffered the consequences. The pattern is still often defended, even by those who were once caned or ridiculed ("It was good for me!"), and something can indeed be said for it. Under punitive sanctions many students acquire techniques of self-control which carry over into higher education. This was true when universities were little more than libraries, and when only those who did not need to be taught acquired an education. When universities began to teach,

[1] Skinner, B. F. *The technology of teaching.* New York: Appleton-Century-Crofts, 1969. Pp. 111–112.

punitive sanctions were added, and it is still true that most college students, whatever their professed ambitions or long-term goals, go to lectures and read textbooks largely to avoid the consequences of not doing so. Let those who disagree look at the evidence to be found in the average student's response to an occasional relaxation of sanctions (an unexpected holiday or reduced assignment, for example) or at the anxiety characteristically associated with examinations. (And let those who still disagree beware of the Idols of the School!)

Aversive control is not easily justified in a democratic society, however, and there are many other reasons why humane efforts have been made to find alternatives. Teachers have naturally preferred that their students should learn without being coerced and that they should even enjoy their studies. The learning that occurs in daily life seems to show these features. Why not bring the real world into the classroom and throw away the birch rod? Arrange conditions under which the student can do what he wants or likes to do rather than what he has to do.

This is undoubtedly a step in the right direction, but it has been misunderstood and misrepresented. The punitive conditions are contrived by teachers, but nonpunitive conditions in the real world are natural. What began as a change from coercion to positive inducement seemed to emerge as a change in the role of the teacher. The teacher could find things to interest the student; he could guide his development; he could be part of his natural social environment; but he could not teach. The real world would do the teaching. The teacher could only help the student learn.

Was this not an unexpected gain? Would the real world not be more likely to produce naturally effective behavior? An appeal to nature is always compelling, and it is still a strong theme in educational philosophy. It appears to challenge the notion of teaching as the transmission of what others already know. What the student learns from contact with the real world is jeopardized when the teacher interferes or meddles with the natural process. There must be no intervention.

Unfortunately, the real world cannot bear the strain which is thus imposed upon it. Not much can be learned from it in one short lifetime. The natural environment has more variety than a badly designed classroom, but it is nevertheless still repetitious, and personal contact with it is limited in scope. When teachers abandoned aversive practices, they lost control. They discarded some subjects and postponed others until the students were "ready" for them. There is a similar effect in higher education. Coverage is reduced when the explicit transmission of knowledge is minimized. The *relevant* world also lacks scope.

What is learned from real life is also faulty. It is well known that the first effect of a natural environment in building athletic or artistic skills often proves troublesome at later stages; the coach or teacher must suppress early natural forms of responding if a final performance is to be perfected. There are intellectual parallels. Outstanding achievements have, no doubt, often been the culmination of a natural process of development, but it is because the instances are so rare that we call them outstanding, and it is perhaps just because they are the exception that we attribute them to genius rather than to outside help.

The physical environment teaches awkward behavior as readily as skilled; the social environment teaches aggression and competition as readily as good will and cooperation; in both worlds, adventitious consequences breed superstition. The real world is strongly punitive, and we are as likely to escape from many parts of it as we are to play hooky from school. All these features have parallels in the world of books. The student may not learn much if he reads only books of current interest; what he learns may be useless or untrue; and bookish knowledge may be largely adventitious. Certainly, vast numbers of students learn to stay away from books altogether as soon as they are free to do so.

Turning students over to the things which currently interest them does not solve the motivational problems that arise in dispensing with overtly punitive methods. It is essentially the abandonment of teaching. There is a much more promising way to remove punitive techniques from the classroom—including the easily concealed aversive features of college instruction—without abandoning the transmission of the culture or the communication of what has already been learned by others. The alternative is surprisingly simple, and I have no doubt that the historian can find many early statements. The problem is not, however, to state an alternative, but to put it into general practice, and we are only now in a position to do so. Recent advances in our understanding of human behavior supply not only the means, but the confidence needed to make significant changes.

We need to replace contrived punitive conditions with contrived alternatives, rather than with the natural alternatives to be found in the current "relevant" environment. The alternative to punishment is what the layman calls reward, but lay usage has long obscured an important detail. Behavior is indeed modified by its consequences, whether rewarding or punishing, but the important thing is *the way in which a consequence is contingent upon behavior.* The prescriptions of the Utilitarians never worked because they emphasized the consequences (pleasure and pain), while neglecting the contingent relations. Under what conditions and at what moment is an act followed by a pleasurable or painful consequence?

The experimental analysis of behavior is concerned with the contingent relations which prevail among three things—the situation in which behavior occurs, the behavior itself, and its rewarding or reinforcing consequences. Extremely complex and subtle contingencies are set up in the laboratory and their effects studied. The results have suggested alternatives to both the punitive sanctions of traditional education and practices in which teaching is turned over to the real world.

A simple contingency of reinforcement in primary or secondary education—such as a token economy or a credit-point system in a classroom—may seem like nothing more than reward in the traditional sense. This is true because the reinforcers have been made as conspicuous as possible in order to make them more clearly contingent upon behavior. To bring a disrupted classroom under control or to replace a punitive environment as quickly as possible, simple and conspicuous consequences may be needed. But higher education clearly calls for something else.

The traditional instrument through which one person benefits from the experience of another is a book, and what is called a textbook is designed to work as expeditious a change as possible. But why should a student read a book or study a textbook? The possibility is worth considering that his behavior in doing so is a simple function of the clarity and frequency of the reinforcing consequences. But what are those consequences? Traditionally, he discovers the extent to which he has understood what he has read from the grade he receives on a test, but a grade is not contingent on behavior in an effective way. Unless the material is itself reinforcing because it is currently of interest, which it cannot always be, he will presumably read, if at all, only to avoid the aversive consequences of a low grade. Much more immediate positive consequences need to be contrived.

The traditional concept of reward suggests something extrinsic to the behavior itself, and it is true that we could reward correct responses to passages in a book with, for example, money—with, say, the remission of parts of a fee paid at the beginning of a course. But nothing so crude is needed. A student is presumably in college to "get an education," and progress in doing so is itself reinforcing. The only requirement is that progress should be conspicuous. A student will continue to read a book if there is evidence that he is undergoing a significant change, that he is increasingly better able to do and say things, that he is progressing toward the completion of the book or the course of which it is a part or the curriculum of which the course is a part. For students whose behavior is not thus reinforced, other reinforcers must be found, but, in general, students can be induced to read—attentively and with pleasure—by making sure that the consequences are immediate, clear cut, and frequent. And what holds for reading holds for other parts of the educational assignment. The necessary conditions can be most easily met if—

1. The student moves at his own pace. Differences in the rate at which students work may be genetic or environmental and are probably both. Of importance, however, is not the source of the differences, but the solution of the problems they raise. A student who is forced to go too fast misses many reinforcing consequences and, indeed, misses more and more of them as he falls further and further behind. A student who could move faster but is held back is not receiving reinforcements which lie within his range. The principle of individual pacing is as applicable to graduate instruction as to teaching in the first grade.

2. The student should not merely "soak up information"; he should respond, and his responses should be immediately evaluated so that successful responses will be reinforced.

3. The student should move through the material in such a

way that what he has just learned helps him to take the next step. Signs of increasing power are important reinforcers. Reinforcement will be maximized if he masters each stage before moving on.

There are readers who will strongly resent these references to behavioral processes in a discussion of higher education, and, unfortunately, only those who have had some firsthand experience with operant conditioning will be easily persuaded of their relevance. But it is no longer a matter of theory. Instructional systems which observe these principles have been designed and tested and have been conspicuously successful in inducing students to study energetically, carefully, and with pleasure. What is learned need not be relevant to their current life; it can therefore be selected to be relevant to their futures. Under these conditions students are less likely to move to escape from education—not only in minor ways such as being inattentive or forgetful, but by taking time off or dropping out of school or college altogether.

Good programmed instruction observes these principles, and a good program is a dramatic demonstration of their power. It is an extraordinarily useful device in acquiring knowledge of a new field in an expeditious way. But the exigencies of contemporary higher education often call for a more thoroughgoing restructuring of practice, and the Personalized System Instruction originated by Fred S. Keller is an outstanding example of what can be done. A recent report evaluating the system with respect to science teaching describes the procedure as follows:

> A student beginning a Keller course finds that the course work is divided into topics or units. In a simple case, the content of the units may correspond to chapters of the course text. At the start of a course, the student receives a printed study guide to direct his work on the first unit. Although study guides vary, a typical one introduces the unit, states objectives, suggests study procedures, and lists study questions. The student may work anywhere—including the classroom—to achieve the objectives outlined in the study guide.
>
> Before moving on to the second unit in the sequence, the student must demonstrate his mastery of the first by perfect or near-perfect performance on a short examination.

He is examined on the unit only when he feels adequately prepared, and he is not penalized for failure to pass a first, second, or later examination. When the student demonstrates mastery of the first unit, he is given the study guide for the next unit. He thus moves through the course at his own pace. He may meet all course requirements before the term is half through or he may require more than a term for completing the course.[2]

Thousands of courses are now being given on the Keller Plan in the United States, South America, and elsewhere. Adjustments to local conditions may have to be made concerning scheduling, grading, and the logistics of material, space, and record-keeping, but the essential features can be preserved. Such a course covers standard material, but covers it much more thoroughly while avoiding most, if not all, of the aversive features of traditional practices. At any given time, the student knows where he stands—what he has done and still has to do—and the same information is available to the instructor and useful to him for different reasons.

Such a course may be constantly improved, since, as in other kinds of instructional programs and in contrast with traditional texts and lectures, weak points can be easily spotted and corrected. Overall modes of presentation will no doubt continue to be improved as experience dictates, but it has already been established that the so-called motivational problem in higher education can be solved in this way. An environment can be constructed in which the student has abundant reasons for studying, and for mastering material, even when it is not currently relevant to his personal problems or interests. It is therefore possible for education to enable new members of a group to profit from what other members have already learned—and in a highly expeditious way.

I suspect that to some these will appear to be words of a philistine. But the position seems to me not only defensible, but inescapable. Must we not ask educators and philosophers of education to state as clearly as possible the observable differences between students who have had and who have not had a "higher education"?

[2] Kulik, J., Kulik, C., and Carmichael, K. The Keller Plan in science teaching. *Science*, 1974, *183*, 381–383. (Also see *The Keller Plan Handbook* by Fred S. Keller and J. Gilmour Sherman, published in 1974 by W. A. Benjamin, Inc., Menlo Park, Cal.)

And should they not say how education is to convert one into the other? I submit that the purposes and goals of education most often set forth in traditional discussions have suggested useful practices, but have masked an unwillingness to be specific about these basic issues.

Of course it is important to stimulate the student's "natural curiosity," but curiosity is of little avail if the student looks only at the world about him. If in our efforts to stimulate curiosity we sacrifice the transmission of what other curious people have already discovered, we deny the student access to an immense world lying beyond his immediate reach.

Of course it is important that the student be creative and imaginative, but if, in making absolutely sure that he is not being imitative, we ignore or conceal the creative achievements of others, we deny him the chance to play a role in a creative process reaching far beyond his own lifetime. The creative achievements of the past have come from men who for the most part, as Newton said of himself, "stood on the shoulders of giants." It is no service to the student to insist that he stand with his feet firmly planted on solid ground.

Sooner or later a discussion of the goals of education turns to ethics and morals, and it is precisely here that the appeal to a natural process of growth is most damaging. That part of a culture which unquestionably demands transmission is its ethical and moral practices. People are not ethical or moral by nature, nor do they simply grow ethical or moral. It is the ethical and moral sanctions maintained by other members of a group which induce them to behave in ethical and moral ways. To leave ethical and moral behavior to the natural endowment of the individual and a natural process of growth is to promote ethical and moral chaos. We must accept that a culture *imposes* its ethical and moral standards upon its members. It can do nothing else.

In more general terms, we must also accept that in transmitting a culture, education *imposes* what has already been learned by others upon its students. To a considerable extent it must decide in advance what a student is to learn. Current philosophies of education spring in part from an unwillingness to take on this responsibility. Educational policy-makers are unwilling to specify what is worth knowing, and once again they leave the decision to the student. But the student is in no position to specify what will ultimately be useful. This is obvious when he is beginning the study of a large field, such as biology or physics, but it is equally true as he enters upon a broader "education for life." Personal idiosyncrasies certainly need to be taken into account, and a program which yielded regimentation and uniformity would be bad educational design, but there are sources of regimentation and uniformity in programs which leave decisions to students, too. We should not be misled because students are readier than we are to accept the responsibility of designing their programs, because their readiness may spring only from current satisfactions.

Those who let students themselves decide what they are to study and leave teaching to the physical, social, and textual environments are essentially abdicating as teachers. They betray students who already care about their future, and fail to help those who have never had any reason to care. It is possible that education will someday be held responsible for the millions of young people who are now not only not well prepared for the future, but not even sure that they have one.

PART IV

A MISCELLANY

13 *The Shaping of Phylogenic Behavior*

14 *The Force of Coincidence*

15 *Reflections on Meaning and Structure*

16 *Walden (One) and Walden Two*

17 *Freedom and Dignity Revisited*

18 *Freedom at Last, From the Burden of Taxation*

13

The Shaping
of Phylogenic Behavior

An unusual topography of operant behavior can often be shaped by making the contingencies of reinforcement increasingly more complex. In a simple demonstration a box is divided into two parts by a low wall, and a hungry rat is placed on one side and food on the other. The rat possesses an initial repertoire of responses (climbing and jumping), some of which take it over the wall and are reinforced by food. As a result, responses having the required topography are strengthened and soon occur on later occasions. If the wall is then made slightly higher, only some of these responses will be successful, but they will begin to occur more frequently, and as a result new topographies of response will appear, which will meet even more demanding contingencies when the height of the wall is again increased. If the height is not increased too rapidly (if some responses are always successful), a very energetic and skill-ful repertoire will result. The rat will eventually go over a wall that it would never cross if it had not been exposed to such a program.

A similar result could be obtained by genetic selection. Rats which most readily or successfully crossed a wall of a given height could be selected for breeding to produce a population among which some members would be more likely to cross a higher wall; and the process could then be repeated. Two strains of hooded rats used in some early genetic experiments at the old Bussey Institute at Harvard University could be separated instantly by putting them one at a time in a shallow box; members of one strain quickly escaped, while members of the other strain remained in the box indefinitely. From the observed facts alone, it was impossible to tell whether the difference was due to operant conditioning, following some such procedure as just described, or a genetic characteristic. When ontogenic shaping can be ruled out, it is standard practice to infer that genetic selection has been responsible for an observed difference of this sort.

The behavior of homing to a fixed site raises similar questions. An organism can be taught to home through operant conditioning by repeatedly placing it in positions from which returning to a fixed site is reinforced. The field may be progressively enlarged, subject only to the limits imposed by the available time and the locomotive capacities of the organism. A parallel process in which contingencies of survival replace contingencies of reinforcement is usually inferred in order to explain, for example, the behavior of bats in leaving and returning to a cave. As the size of the original group increased, those bats which went farther and farther afield to obtain food and returned successfully were presumably more likely to survive and breed and transmit the behavior.

Contingencies of reinforcement which shape ontogenic behavior can be arranged and studied in the laboratory. Most of the contingencies of survival responsible for phylogenic behavior observed in the field are merely inferred. But some evidence of environmental conditions which probably changed in such a way as to shape complex phylogenic behavior has emerged in connection with the theory of continental drift and the spreading of the sea floor.

An example which has recently attracted attention is the behavior of the green turtle (*Chelonia mydas*), which feeds in the water pastures along the coast of Brazil and swims more than a thousand miles to breed on Ascension Island. The journey takes several weeks and demonstrates remarkable navigational skills, since a five-mile target must be hit after about one thousand miles of travel in the open sea. As Carr [1] has argued, it is hard to imagine that behavior as complex as this could have evolved through natural selection under the present circumstances. In 1964, Fraser [2] pointed out that 150 million years ago the turtles "would have only a narrow arm of the sea to negotiate; for since the ancient latitudes of Rio Doce and the projection of Ascension on the African coast are in precise agreement, the nesting ground was lying there just across the water, a mere hundred miles or so from its land based home among the elephant grass of east Brazil."

The case is not quite that simple, however, as Carr and Coleman [3] have recently pointed out. Ascension Island is a relatively late member of a chain of volcanic islands which have appeared as the sea floor spread. The turtles may first have gone to islands close to Brazil, but these slowly submerged. They presumably then went on to more distant islands in the same general direction, of which Ascension was the last to appear. The fact remains that the behavior of feeding along the shores of Brazil and swimming to a breeding ground relatively safe from predators met progressively more demanding conditions as the distances increased, either continuously or in a step-wise fashion.

Another program of contingencies of survival resulting from the spreading of the sea floor may explain the behavior of American and European freshwater eels, which appear to have a common spawning ground in the Sargasso Sea. It was Alfred Wegener, the father of the theory of continental drift, who noted the relevance of this fact to his theory, in the fourth edition of his *Origin of continents and oceans*.[4] The point was suggested to him, as early as 1922, by J. Schmidt. Schmidt's early research [5] showed that the European eel (*Anguilla anguilla*) breeds in an area northeast and north of the West Indies. The young eels in the larval stage (called

---

[1] Carr, A. Adaptive aspects of the scheduled travel of *Chelonia*. In *Animal orientation and navigation*. Corvallis: Oregon State University Press, 1966.

[2] Fraser, R. *Understanding the earth*. New York: Penguin, 1964.

[3] Carr, A. and Coleman, P. J. Seafloor spreading theory and the odyssey of the green turtle. *Nature*, 1974, *249*, 128–130.

[4] Wegener, A. *The origin of continents and oceans* (4th ed.). 1929. (English translation, New York: Dover, 1966).

[5] Schmidt, J. *Nature*, 1923, *111*, 51–54.

leptocephali) are small and leaflike in appearance. They rise to the surface and with the help of the Gulf Stream move toward Europe. Year-old larvae are to be found in the mid-Atlantic and as far east as the Azores; two-year-old larvae are found on the shores of Europe and in the Mediterranean; and after three years they undergo metamorphosis and appear as elvers in freshwater streams, where they mature. Years later the mature eels return to the place in which they were hatched. As the sea floor spread, the spawning ground moved much farther from European rivers than from American, and Wegener credits H. Osterwald with realizing that "the gradual drift of this ocean basin plus America away from Europe" explains the fact that the larval stage of the European eel is three years while that of the American is only one.

In 1969 the present author pointed out the possible relevance of the spreading of the sea floor to the shaping of the phylogenic behavior of the eel.[6] The behavior is truly remarkable. From the breeding ground to the mouth of the Nile, for example, a young eel in the larval stage travels, as Schmidt pointed out, about 6,000 miles in a period of three years. Ocean currents will explain only part of this migration. The mature eel makes a return journey of the same distance against the current. As with the green turtle, it is hard to believe that their extraordinary behavior could have arisen from natural selection under present environmental conditions. But if the distances were at first short, and if they increased *no more than a few inches each generation,* as the theory of continental drift implies, then some members of each generation could have satisfied the new contingencies and bred to transmit the behavior.

In 1948 Wolfson[7] argued that "continental drift was the stimulus for the evolution of the more highly developed forms of migration [of birds]." He stated his hypothesis in four steps:

(a) Before the advent of continental drift many birds were performing short flights between breeding and feeding areas.

(b) With the onset of drift these areas diverged slowly.

---

[6] Skinner, B. F. *Contingencies of reinforcement: A theoretical analysis.* New York: Appleton-Century-Crofts, 1969. (See Chap. 7).

[7] Wolfson, A. Bird migration and the concept of continental drift. *Science,* 1948, *108,* 23–30.

(c) The birds continued their use of these areas because of their well-developed homing instincts.

(d) As the distances increased, only those individuals that had the necessary sources of energy for the flight survived.

Wolfson pointed to the fact that, for example, the Arctic tern, which breeds in northern North America and migrates to the Antarctic, first flies *eastward* across the Atlantic to Europe and then southward along the African coast. The eastward journey may at first have been very short, but as the continents separated, successive generations would have flown slightly greater distances and what seems now like a nonadaptive flight pattern is thus explained.

North Atlantic salmon show a pattern which is the reverse of that of the eel; they breed in freshwater rivers but live most of their adult lives in the ocean. They also show a long east-west migration that could have been shaped by the separation of the continents. According to Orr,[8] "American Atlantic salmon have been taken on the West Coast of Greenland, and those from Sweden have also been recorded there, a distance of almost 3,000 miles from the home streams of both." At one time the distances were very much shorter, and navigation must have been scarcely more than a matter of moving along a coastline.

A different effect of the plate tectonics related to continental drift may have produced contingencies of survival which shaped certain features of the behavior of salmon on the West Coast. Columbia River salmon, for example, breed in shallow, relatively still fresh water, with a gravel base, but spend most of their lives in the Pacific Ocean, particularly in the Gulf of Alaska. At the present time the mature salmon reach suitable breeding grounds only by fighting their way up through treacherous rapids and waterfalls. At an earlier stage in the development of the river, however, suitable breeding conditions may have been found close to shore. At that time the salmon need not have possessed any of the extraordinarily skillful and powerful behavior with which they now conquer the hazardous flow of the river. As the river matured, suitable breeding grounds should have receded from the shore, setting up a program of contingencies of survival which shaped the present behavior,

[8] Orr, R. T. *Animals in migration.* New York: Macmillan, 1970.

each generation being required to meet contingencies only very slightly more difficult than the preceding.

Phylogenic shaping of behavior is plausible, of course, only if the species, or at least some recognizable earlier form, was in existence when the geological change occurred. The green turtle, the eel, and migrating birds seem to meet this requirement, and Professor P. J. Coleman (personal communication) has pointed out that "the Western seaboard is a geologically young entity and a development of the west flowing rivers is certainly within the time span of the salmon group as it is recognized today."

A continuous shaping process, in both ontogenic and phylogenic behavior, has been only slowly recognized. Wegener and Schmidt pointed to the breeding practices of the eel mainly to support the theory of continental drift. Wolfson emphasized the selection of birds capable of flying greater distances and pointed out that the *path* of flight was more significant than the *extent* in supporting an explanation in terms of continental drift, but he assumed that birds followed such a path because of a homing instinct. Fraser drew on conclusions from the lengthening voyage of the green turtle, but Carr [9] emphasized the importance of evidence "bearing on probable paleolithic conditions at the time of origin, *or of refinement,* of each pattern [of island-finding behavior]" (italics added). Carr argued that "any female with the urge and capacity to go out to the island will contribute more genes to reinforce the island breeding pattern in the race. Each generation, more turtles go out to the island simply because their genotype was made more prevalent by the island-seeking tendency of the preceding generation. The island-seeking migration is thus a successful evolutionary venture, and has become the established regimen for the population."

It is this genotype which changed under selection as the continents moved apart. Carr and Coleman speak of the repetitive extension of previous travel paths and suggest that "the process of racial learning is of the repetitive, stepping-stone type, which requires no radical change in behavior at any point."

It is possible to be a little more specific. The shaping of

[9] *Op. cit.*

phylogenic behavior, like the shaping of ontogenic behavior, involves at least three things:

1. Behavior comes under the control of new stimuli. In the phylogenic case this could involve extensive changes in sense organs, but it also involves the development of particular forms of stimulus control which, as in the ontogenic case, do not require changes in sensitivity. Shaping usually involves a shift in the range of controlling stimuli. When a stimulus which is not central to an existing range acquires special controlling power (either through genetic selection or operant reinforcement), a new range emerges in which new stimuli are now for the first time effective and can be strengthened to produce a range differing still further from the original. Thus, if an unusual visual pattern becomes particularly effective, new patterns even more unusual begin to exert control and are subject to further selection as the contingencies change.

A distinction is often made in discussing homing behavior or migration between "knowing where to go" and "knowing how to find the way," but the concept of knowledge causes trouble. The organism begins to migrate or home by responding to current stimuli; some of its responses may produce other stimuli which then take over. In following a long path the organism may be under the control of a succession of discrete stimuli or such a sustained stimulus as that used in celestial navigation. (The present argument does not, unfortunately, throw any light on the stimuli which actually exert control, although the search for such stimuli may be aided by a consideration of the probable requirements in earlier stages of the shaping process).

2. The topography of behavior changes. In phylogenic behavior this may involve elaborate changes in the strength and mode of operation of effectors, but it also involves changes in the effective topography of a stable system, as in the ontogenic case. Shaping usually involves a shift in the range of effective topographies. When an unusual form of response is strengthened by genetic selection or operant conditioning, new forms may appear for the first time which can in turn be strengthened as the contingencies change.

3. Easily overlooked is a third effect of shaping—a mainte-

nance of, or an increase in, the probability that behavior having a given topography and under the control of given stimuli will actually occur. The effect on probability is due, in phylogenic behavior, to the selection of genotypes and, in ontogenic behavior, to operant conditioning. The tendency to behave in a given way upon a given occasion has been attributed to instinct in the phylogenic case and habit in the ontogenic case. In both it has been associated with the concept of purpose, and in ontogenic behavior with expectation or intention. Concepts of this sort add nothing to the observed facts, and they cause trouble because, by appearing to refer to inner determiners of behavior, they often serve as substitutes for the further explanation which will eventually be provided by physiology.

It is not necessary to refer to underlying structures or functions in order to study the way in which an organism inherits a tendency to behave in a given way in the presence of given stimuli, but the physiology will, it is hoped, eventually be understood. What evolves is an organism as a physical system, and it is such an organism that is modified by operant conditioning. We do not know whether the physiological changes which occur in the shaping of phylogenic behavior are similar to those which occur in operant conditioning. Certainly, there are vast differences in the conditions under which the two processes occur. It is not impossible, however, that operant conditioning, itself an evolved feature of an organism, should have utilized a physiological system which had already been developed in natural selection.

14

The Force of Coincidence

In the grade school that I attended as a child, a single teacher taught two grades in the same room. While one class recited, the other worked on its assignments. One day in third grade, when my teacher was talking with the other class, I raised my hand, waved it wildly to attract her attention, and said "I was *reading* the word 'middle' just when you *said* it." Both classes laughed. I had been impressed by the coincidence, but I should have been impressed by the fact that I was impressed.

The current revolt against reason and science has made much of psychic phenomena, such as precognition in dreams and extra-sensory perception, and various transcendental states of conscious-ness. In his book *The Roots of Coincidence* [1] Arthur Koestler has discussed another kind of evidence said to be neglected by the scientific establishment: things happen which cannot be explained "by the laws of chance." After the book was published many people wrote to him to report additional strange coincidences, and a

[1] Koestler, A. *The roots of coincidence.* New York: Random House, 1972.

second volume is, I believe, to appear containing further data. The evidence cuts both ways. It shows that there are many coincidences which are hard to explain, but it also shows that coincidences attract an unusual amount of attention and are long remembered.

Coincidence is the heart of operant conditioning. A response is strengthened by certain kinds of consequences, but not necessarily because they are actually produced by it. Indeed, it is quite unlikely that a behavioral process could have evolved which took into account the *manner* in which a response produces an effect. There are too many reasons why consequences follow behavior, and they depend on features of the environment which are too unstable to play any part in natural selection. But since an event which follows another event is likely enough to have been caused by it, coincidence suffices.

That solution to the problem of causality is not, however, free of trouble. It means that behavior may be strengthened by merely adventitious consequences, and such behavior is not likely to be useful. Vulnerability to coincidence must have increased as the process of operant conditioning accelerated, and when a single instance of response-and-consequence began to work a significant change, various kinds of superstitious behavior were inevitable. The more "intelligent" the organism, the more likely it was to be superstitious. Moreover, superstitious behavior is often self-perpetuating and even self-enhancing. Recovery from a self-limited illness, for example, reinforces any therapeutic action a person may take, and since he is therefore more likely to take it again when ill, it is likely to be adventitiously reinforced again and hence further strengthened.

The fact that two basic types of superstitious behavior are commonly observed in such an "unintelligent" organism as a pigeon [2,3] suggests that superstition must have been very widespread before corrective measures were developed. Such measures are, of course, now common. When a response appears to have had an unlikely consequence, a fairly characteristic move is to repeat it

[2] Skinner, B. F. 'Superstition' in the pigeon. *Journal of Experimental Psychology*, 1948, *38*, 168–172.

[3] Morse, W. H. and Skinner, B. F. A second type of superstition in the pigeon. *American Journal of Psychology*, 1957, *70*, 308–311.

immediately. If the same consequence follows, the response is further strengthened. (Using essentially a synonym for "reinforced," we say it is "confirmed.") If the same response does not follow (as is likely to be the case if the first was adventitious), the acquired strength is lost through extinction and subsequent behavior is then "in better touch with reality."

It is possible that people learn to test the causal efficacy of their behavior simply because they are then more likely to be consistently reinforced, but more complex tests of the significance of consequences are usually acquired from others. Someone must devise each test for the first time, but no one person could devise many of them within a single lifetime. Most people probably learn even the simplest measures from others.

This is all part of the field of self-knowledge and self-management, and it is almost wholly a social product. It is only when other people ask "Why did you do that?" that we begin to examine the contingencies responsible for our behavior. As a simple operant we open a window because we then get fresh air, but it is only when someone asks "Why?" that we describe the relation between our behavior and its consequences, as by saying "I opened the window because fresh air then came in." The sequence is taken to be sufficient evidence. Recent power failures turned up a number of stories of people who described them as adventitious consequences in the same way. A small boy walking along the street striking trees and picket fences with a stick happens to strike an electric light pole, or a housewife happens to plug in an iron, just as all the lights in the city go out, and both may report, and under certain social circumstances may insist, that they have caused the trouble.

The physical facts which explain why fresh air comes in through an open window or why plugging in an iron blows a fuse or blacks out a city have nothing to do with personal action. As the history of the idea of causality abundantly demonstrates, one thing has often been said to cause another simply because it precedes it—as the operant paradigm seems to imply. A very simple example, involving spatial features, is seen in the kind of settings studied by Michotte.[4] When one black spot moving on a white field approaches another and the other moves away just as contact is made,

---

[4] Michotte, A. *La perception de la causalité*. Paris, 1946.

the first is said to cause the second to move. The first spot "strikes" the second as one billiard ball strikes another. And if we convert spots into living things a whole new realm of causality seems to open. I once made some small "turtles" for a child by pasting Mexican jumping beans on small squares of paper with the corners bent down as legs. The turtles moved about on a plate of glass as the beans "jumped." When one turtle moved toward another just as the other moved away, the child immediately reported that the second turtle had been frightened.

We gain from analyzing the contingencies which affect our behavior—using scientific and statistical methods—in part because we reduce our vulnerability to merely incidental cases, and our gains lead us to continue to do so when the contingencies are superstitious. Many myths appear to represent this function. Any behavior executed just before it begins to rain is strengthened if rain is reinforcing, as it is at the end of a severe drought. And because the more conspicuous the behavior, the more effective the coincidence, an elaborate ritual such as a rain dance may evolve. In an area in which drought is self-limited, people are likely to begin to dance near the end of a drought—when the probability of "reinforcement" is particularly high—and such a superstition is therefore self-perpetuating and even self-enhancing. A person who is asked why he dances may simply reply that rain then soon follows, but if he is asked *why* dancing produces rain, he may answer by generalizing from instances in which similar consequences are not adventitious. Social contingencies offer the richest sources, and the dance may be interpreted as a form of asking for rain or pleasing and hence appeasing someone who is withholding rain.

We dismiss rain dancing as a form of superstition because the adventitious nature of the consequences can be demonstrated "statistically," but we continue to be fascinated by coincidences which are "inexplicable according to the laws of chance." This is likely to be the case so long as we forget that the world in which we live is an extremely complex sample space, in which it is doubtful whether there are any "laws" of chance which apply to many of the single events occurring in it. Coincidences are certainly to be expected, and the sheer number may be felt to build up a case for a force or agent which is metaphysical, supernatural, or at least not part of the current corpus of science. But the mere accumulation of instances has less to do with probability than with the striking force of coincidence.

It is a rare person who picks up a hand of thirteen spades at bridge and views it as no less likely to occur than any of the other hands he has picked up during his experience as a player, or who enjoys a run of luck at roulette without calling it his lucky day or acknowledging his debt to Lady Luck, or who when an honest coin has come heads twenty-five times in a row will not then be more likely to bet on tails. The genetic endowment responsible for our behavioral processes cannot fully protect us from the whims of chance, and the statistical and scientific measures we devise to bring our behavior under the more effective control of nature are not adequate for the extraordinarily complex sample space in which we live. Science has not ignored some underlying order; it has not yet devised ways of protecting us against spurious evidences of order.

15

Reflections on Meaning
and Structure

Th'expense of spirit in a waste of shame
Is lust in action; and till action, lust
Is perjur'd, murd'rous, bloody, full of blame,
Savage, extreme, rude, cruel, not to trust;
Enjoy'd no sooner, but despised straight;
Past reason hunted; and no sooner had,
Past reason hated as a swallow'd bait
On purpose laid to make the taker mad:
Mad in pursuit, and in possession so;
Had, having, and in quest to have, extreme;
A bliss in proof, and prov'd, a very woe;
Before, a joy propos'd; behind, a dream
All this the world well knows; yet none knows well
To shun the heaven that leads men to this hell.

In their detailed analysis of the structure of Shakespeare's Sonnet 129, Jakobson and Jones [1] note that *"and very wo* instead of *a very wo* is an obvious misprint, under the assimilative influences of the antecedent *and* in the same line and in the first two lines of the same quatrain." Having written (or set in type) the word *and* three times in three lines, the poet (or typesetter) wrote (or set) it again although the meaning called for *a.* But what about the third of these four *ands?* Can we be sure that without the first two it would not have been *but,* say, or *yet?* The evidence is clearer in the

---

[1] Jakobson, R., and Jones, L. G. *Shakespeare's verbal art in th' expence of spirit.* The Hague: Mouton, 1970.

fourth instance because *and* is a mistake, but there are presumably
reasons why words are written when they are not mistakes.

An assimilative influence may bear on less than a whole word,
and the fact that *wo* rimes with *so* is an example. Here again the
evidence is better when it explains a blemish. Jakobson and Jones
quote J. M. Robertson to the effect that "collapse recurs when *a
very wo* fades into *a dreame* for the rime's sake" and Edward
Hubler to the effect that "the anticlimactic position of *not to trust*
is owing entirely to the need for a rime." But have we any reason
to suppose that assimilative influences are not at work in rimes
which do not show collapse or anticlimax? In Sonnet 90, for example, in the line *And other strains of wo, which now seem wo*
the second *wo* may be attributed in part to the first and to an
earlier occurrence in riming position in the second quatrain. In a
prose version something closer to *unbearable* might have been more
to the point.

The meaning of other words must also be taken into account.
It is not surprising that one who has been speaking of perjury,
murder, and madness should say *wo,* either through word association or as the effect of a common subject matter. But meaning
raises special problems. Structure has the enormous advantage of
being accessible. The formal properties of Sonnet 129 are not all
immediately obvious, as Jakobson and Jones have convincingly
shown, but once pointed out they are there for everyone to see.
But what are meanings, and where are they to be found? A dictionary does not give the meanings of words, it gives other words
having the same meanings. The meaning of a poem is similarly
elusive. When a person tells us what a poem means to him, he
merely tells us how a meaning might be otherwise expressed. Suppose he paraphrases Sonnet 129 in some such way as this: "Sexual
behavior is both rewarded and punished, and when we enage in it
because of the rewards, we subject ourselves to the punishments. No
one knows what to do about it." This is not one meaning of the
sonnet; it is only one other way of saying what the sonnet says.

To get closer to meaning we should have to look at the circumstances under which the sonnet was written. We cannot do that
with Sonnet 129. We are limited to making a few guesses about
what might have happened to Shakespeare to induce him to write
as he did. It has often been pointed out that the sonnet is bitter.

What could have been so bad about sex? Temporary impotence
(". . . *passion ending, doth the purpose lose"*) is scarcely bad
enough. Social, legal, or religious sanctions may have been "blouddy
full of blame" and could have led Shakespeare to "dispise" himself,
but they are scarcely perjured or murderous. Perhaps the best guess
is the pox, but we shall probably never know. Fortunately, so far
as the present point is concerned, it does not matter. Assume any
plausible set of circumstances; how could they have given rise to a
sonnet?

We gain nothing from supposing that the sonnet first came
into existence in some preverbal form, that circumstances gave rise
to an idea in Shakespeare's mind which he then put into words. If
we begin in that way, we must explain how circumstances give rise
to ideas, and that is much more difficult than explaining how they
give rise to verbal behavior.[2] Certain events in Shakespeare's life
induced him to emit two opposed and seemingly incompatible sets
of responses with respect to sex. The sets are epitomized by *heaven*
and *hell.* When lust is heaven it is a *bliss* and a *joy,* and it is then
hunted and *pursued.* When lust is hell, it is uncouth (*extreame,*
rude), deceptive *(perjured, not to trust),* costly (a *waste,* an *expense*),
demeaning (a thing of *shame,* full of *blame*), and violent (*cruel,*
savage, blouddy, murdrous), and it is then *dispised* and *hated.* The
two sets of responses are not really incompatible, because lust is one
thing or the other depending on the time. Heaven comes first and
hell follows, and this temporal aspect of the circumstances evokes
several pairs of terms *(in action—till action, no sooner—straight, in*
pursuit,—in possession, had—having, and *before—behind.)*

These key expressions, which can be thus arranged in thematic
groups, may be close to the "primordial" verbal material from
which the sonnet was composed. (They were not all necessarily
available when the poet began to write, since associative and assimilative influences could have generated other material as the writing
proceeded.) They are far from being a sonnet, and there is much
about them that any imagined set of circumstances will not easily
explain. Certainly many other responses could have been evoked.
Why this particular selection of synonyms? And what determined

[2] Skinner, B. F. *Verbal behavior.* New York: Appleton-Century-
Crofts, 1957.

the attribution of "parts of speech?" A setting which gave rise to a *waste of shame* could easily have evoked *a shameful waste,* or *shamefully wasted,* or *a shame and a waste.* And what about the order in which the responses occur? Nine adjectives or adjectival phrases were strung together in the first quatrain: *perjurd, murdrous, blouddy, full of blame, savage, extreame, rude, cruel, not to trust.* Why that one order, when 362,879 other orders were possible? And which pair of terms was to go with which indicator of time? Why not *before injoyd, behind dispised?* Or *injoyd in proof, dispised when provd?* And what was to be done about assertion? (Very little was in fact done in Sonnet 129: only the two *is*'s in the first quatrain and the two *know*'s in the couplet assert anything. It is this lack of assertion rather than the lack of "logical organization" of which John Crowe Ransom complains that keeps 129 from being "a true sonnet.")

I have argued (using Sonnet 129 as an example; see note 2) that verbal material is worked over in this way to sharpen and improve the effect on the reader, possibly on the poet himself as his own reader. The point here is simply that at every stage the material will necessarily have form or structure. Even unworked verbal behavior has formal properties, though possibly only as by-products. At that stage it is possible that a poet's philosophy of composition could be expressed in the words of the Duchess: "Take care of the sense and the sounds will take care of themselves." But there are other sources of form or structure.

One is to be found in certain prior specifications. Shakespeare intended a sonnet, and it did not turn to an ode. But what is the role of "intention"? How does a prior specification work? One effect may be severely restrictive. Only topics of a certain size are available to the writer of a sonnet, and they must be developed with phrases of a limited length; only words or sequences of words which fit the iambic meter can be used; the rime scheme must be respected; and so on. Shakespeare did not suffer much from these restrictions. From an extraordinarily rich vocabulary suitable words were available, although some of them puzzled his contemporaries and still puzzle us today. He fudged his grammar (Jakobson and Jones point out that *not to trust* and *To shun the heaven* "seem even to transgress the grammatical standard of the Elizabethan time"). He punctuated ambiguously, so that his sentence structure was often unclear, but possibly therefore more effective. Riding and Graves [3] and Empson [4] have paid particular attention to this device. He was occasionally illogical (why *till* action, when the rest of the sonnet makes it clear that lust is perjurd, murdrous, and so on *after* action?).

We have some evidence of his success in fitting form to subject matter. He packed his lines with different quantities of meaning, and to some extent according to the position of a line in the sonnet. What might be called the density of meaning in each of the fourteen lines in the first hundred sonnets was determined in the following way. To escape from preconceptions about density, a rather mechanical method of scanning was adopted. Each line was first scanned strictly as iambic pentameter: "Bite *to* the *blood* and *burn into* the *bone.*" When the accent fell on a preposition, auxiliary, possessive pronoun, article, copula, or such an ending as -*ness,* -*ing,* -*ance,* or -*ment,* it was shifted forward or backward whenever possible to an adjacent syllable not classified as above and not already included in the scanning; otherwise it was omitted. In the example the accent on *to* was shifted backward to *bite,* but the accent on *to* in *into* could not be shifted because there was no appropriate adjacent syllable and was therefore eliminated. A line of four accented syllables remained. This stage usually yielded four or five stressed syllables per line. Each line was then examined for syllables not yet included which were parts of nouns, verbs, adjectives, and adverbs, and these were added. The result was a scansion which took account of practically every important syllable. The method was arbitrary but yielded a plausible reading in almost every case.

The average numbers of stressed syllables in each of the fourteen lines in the hundred sonnets were then determined. The results are shown in Figure 1, which should be read as if it were the right-hand profile of a sonnet as usually printed, except that length of line is due to "density of meaning" rather than letters and spaces (the couplet not being indented). The average for the three quatrains taken together is almost exactly five syllables. The second line in each quatrain is, however, conspicuously short. Density rises toward the end of the sonnet, and both lines in the couplet are

[3] Riding, L. and Graves, R. *A survey of modernist poetry.* New York, 1928.

[4] Empson, W. *Seven types of ambiguity.* London, 1930.

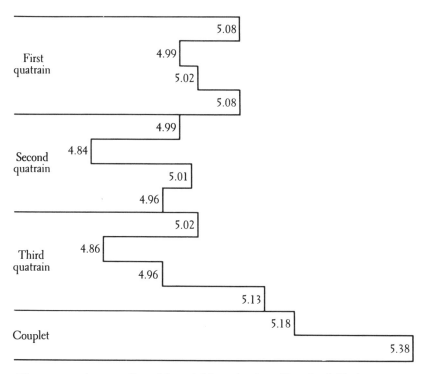

Figure 1 *Average Densities of Lines in One Hundred Shakespeare Sonnets*

The right-hand mean profile, where length of line represents density of meaning rather than number of letters and spaces. The second line in each quatrain tends to be short. Both lines of the couplet contain many meaningful syllables.

denser than any line in the quatrains. The last line is particularly so, as if Shakespeare had fallen behind in making his point and was forced to pack the line tightly. The fact that the couplet often makes a point of its own and has little room in which to do so is probably relevant.

Why should a poet submit to the restrictions imposed by a prior specification of form or structure? Why write sonnets rather than maxims, aphorisms, letters, or short essays? What is gained from dancing in chains? It has been argued that early literature had the form of poetry because it was more easily remembered by those who recited it, and what is easily memorized is likely to be quoted.

A philistine might say that a poet has an eye on public relations. He is concerned with putting his points across and chooses a memorable, quotable form. A philistine might also say that the structure of a poem makes what is said particularly convincing. Are we not more likely to assent to the conclusion of a syllogism if it is expressed in a meter which has been established by the premises and if it ends in a satisfying rime? Things have come out right; why ask whether they are true or false? But there are, of course, better reasons, many of which lie above and beyond prose meanings, although they are not exclusively matters of form or structure.

Formal properties which are not the result of a prior specification arise during the writing of a poem from the formal and thematic "influences" mentioned at the beginning of this paper. Word play is an example. A pun is necessarily a combination of structure and meaning, and even a vague *double-entendre* may be related to structure. *In what form* can one write an opening line that means not only, as a French translation [5] has it, *L'esprit dispersé dans un abîme de honte,* but also, if Jakobson and Jones are right, ejaculation or the "spendings" of nineteenth-century pornography?

Some evidence of the mode of action of an "influence" is available. Form and meaning are both involved in alliteration and assonance. These properties are usually avoided in prose (we rewrite *pour éviter les assonances*) but are accepted in poetry. An excessive predilection for alliteration may have the effect of a prior specification and impose restrictions which are not always successfully evaded, but a moderate use is condoned and valued. It need not be "intentional." The dominant "influence" is formal rather than thematic. After emitting a response having a given sound, the poet is somewhat more likely to emit another response having that sound. The result is a structural feature which lends itself, in some degree, to objective analysis.

Shakespeare's sonnets contain many alliterative lines. To what extent do they show an alliterative tendency? I have reported an attempt to answer that question.[6] The stressed syllables in the first

[5] Jouve, Jean Pierre. *Mercure de France,* May 1, 1955.

[6] Skinner, B. F. The alliteration in Shakespeare's sonnets: A study in literary behavior. *Psychological Record,* 1939, *3,* 186–192.

hundred sonnets were determined in the manner described above, their initial sounds were examined, and lines containing no instances of a given sound, or one, two, three, or four instances were counted. The results were compared with the numbers of lines to be expected from chance, as calculated with a binomial expansion. The conclusions of that study were summarized as follows:

> *Lines containing four like initial consonants.*
> (Ex.: *B*orne on the *b*ier with white and *b*ristly *b*eard.)
> Of these lines there are only eight more than would be expected from chance, and four of these are due to the repetition of the same word or words. Not more than once in twenty-five sonnets (350 lines) does Shakespeare lengthen a series of three like consonants into four, except when he repeats a word.
> *Lines containing three like initial consonants.*
> (Ex.: *S*ave that my *s*oul's imaginary *s*ight.)
> Of these lines there are thirty-three too many, but twenty-nine of these are due to repetition of the same word. Only four are, therefore, "pure" alliteration. Except when he repeated a whole word, Shakespeare changed a line of two like consonants into one of three not oftener than once in twenty-five sonnets.
> *Lines containing two like initial consonants.*
> There are ninety-two excess lines of this sort, but the correction for repetition gives a *shortage* of approximately forty lines. Allowing for eight lines extended to contain three or four occurrences, we may say that once in about every three sonnets Shakespeare *discarded* a word because its initial consonant had already been used.

Jakobson and Jones note the presence of this kind of structural feature in Sonnet 129: "Each line displays a conspicuous alliteration or repetition of sound sequences and entire morphemes or words." But can we be sure that roughly the same alliteration would not have occurred if Shakespeare had drawn his words out of a hat? The result is not a statistical artifact. A similar study of Wordsworth showed, as one might expect, that he discarded many of the alliterative words which must have turned up as he wrote. In a poet like Swinburne on the other hand, alliteration is statistically conspicuous.

In a study of Swinburne's alliteration [7] the initial consonants in the stressed syllables of 500 lines of *Atalanta in Calydon* were examined. Instances were counted in which a sound was followed by the same sound in the next syllable, in the next syllable but one, in the next syllable but two, and so on. These observed frequencies were converted into percentages of the expected frequencies calculated from the total number of sounds. (No correction was made for the repetition of whole words.) The results are shown in Figure 2. When Swinburne uses a stressed initial sound, he shows a strong tendency to use it again in the next syllable, a slightly weaker tendency to use it in the next but one, and so on, the tendency remaining statistically significant for four syllables. The open circles show insignificant differences.

Figure 2 also shows a similar tabulation for Shakespeare. If there is any alliteration in these hundred sonnets, it is confined to successive syllables, and even there it is largely a matter of repeated whole words. (Some instances of repetition follow from Puttenham "redoubles" or "translacers," in which a word or root at the end of a line is repeated at the beginning of the next line. There are at least six of these in the first hundred sonnets.)

Writing under the control of prior specifications must be called "intentional." Only passages are allowed to stand which have the effect of fulfilling the conditions of a contract. Nevertheless, the first person who wrote three quatrains and added a couplet, all on a single theme, did not "intend" to write an English sonnet. If he found the result pleasing, however, he may have written other poems with similar structural properties, which at some point must have begun to act as a set of rules: to produce a particular kind of literary effect write three quatrains and add a couplet, all in iambic pentameter. The structural features which result from formal and thematic processes are not basically intentional (that is, they are not introduced by the writer because of their effects), but if the effects are pleasing, the writer may take steps to give these processes greater play.

Where should we place the structural properties pointed out

[7] Skinner, B. F. A quantitative estimate of certain types of sound-patterning in poetry. *American Journal of Psychology*, 1941, *54*, 64–79.

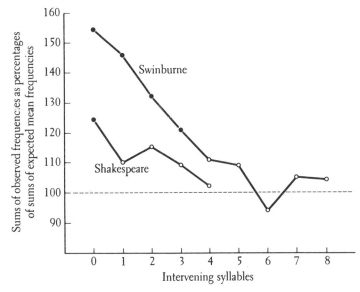

Figure 2 *The Alliterative Spans of Shakespeare and Swinburne*

The point at zero for Swinburne should be read as follows: "In 500 lines of *Atalanta in Calydon* the number of successive stressed syllables beginning with the same sound is 154 percent of the number expected from chance." The percentage declines but remains significant even when syllables are separated by three intervening syllables. The figure for Shakespeare is about 124 percent, but much of this is due to the repetition of whole words.

by Jakobson and Jones? Are they "negligible accidents governed by the rule of chance," [8] are they generated by formal and thematic verbal processes, or are they the fulfillment of prior specifications? The extent to which the features of Sonnet 129 are to be found in the other sonnets is relevant. In a purely physical sense every sonnet has a center, and one moves toward it in reading the first half and away from it in reading the second half; the first seven lines in every sonnet are therefore centripetal and the last centrifugal. The terminal couplet is necessarily "asymmetrically contrasted" with the non-terminal quatrains. But other features are quite idiosyncratic.

[8] Jakobson, R. Subliminal verbal patterning in poetry. *Studies in General and Oriental Linguistics,* Tokyo, 1970 (Quoted by Richards in reference 9).

Of how many of the sonnets can it be said that "the odd strophes in contradistinction to the inner ones abound in substantives and adjectives"? Or that "the outer strophes carry a higher syntactic rank than the inner ones"? Or that "the anterior strophes show an internal alteration of definite and indefinite articles"? Or that "the terminal couplet opposes concrete and primary nouns to the abstract and/or deverbative nouns of the quatrains"? Or that "each of the six initial lines displays a grammatical parallelism of its two hemistichs"?

Idiosyncratic or not, accidental or not, the features are there, and we should perhaps turn from the conditions which may have produced them to their effect on the reader. Jakobson and Jones insist that this "amazing external and internal structuralism [is] palpable to any responsive and unprejudiced reader"; but Richards certainly comes closer to the truth when he says that Sonnet 129 "is now shown to have a degree of exactly describable structural order which—could it have been pointed out to them in such precise unchallengeable detail—would certainly have thrown Shakespeare himself along with his most intent and admiring readers into deeply wondering astonishment," [9] and Jakobson has referred to "subliminal structure," as if it were out of reach of direct observation, and to "deep structure," as if it could be reached only through a penetrating analysis. Certainly the reader need not be aware of the structural features of a poem in order to enjoy it. The effect of music on a listener is due to its structure, since there is nothing else to have an effect, but few listeners—even those who are "most intent and admiring"—know anything about the structure of music and can see it only with difficulty when it is pointed out.

The visibility of structure is particularly important to the writer, who is his own first and most important reader. A writer accepts some of the verbal responses which occur to him and rejects others. He puts those he accepts into some kind of effective order, he adds grammatical tags, he asserts or denies the result, and so on. To do this he must see what he has written—the simple physical structure of his verbal behavior. Moreover, he may learn to write in given ways because what he sees pleases him. Richards has sug-

[9] Richards, I. A. Jakobson's Shakespeare: The subliminal structures of a sonnet. *Times Literary Supplement,* May 28, 1970.

gested "traceable linkages" between Jakobson's work and recent genetics, and I have raised the question of a different genetic linkage elsewhere.[10] The effect on the reader—particularly on the writer as reader—is important because a poem evolves under a kind of natural selection. All behavior is intimately affected by its consequences, and just as the conditions of selection are more important in the evolution of a species than the mutations, so the selective action of a pleasing effect is more important than the meaningful sources of the responses selected. Pleasing responses survive as a poem evolves.

Whether or not the structure of a poem is "subliminal" has a bearing on this issue. (The linguist's "deep structure," like Freud's "depth psychology," is a spatial metaphor which serves several functions. It is useful in referring to the visibility of behavioral processes and their effects and to the role played by visibility in the determination of behavior. It should not, of course, be used to suggest that an analysis is profound rather than superficial.) Richards has pointed to a useful distinction between two kinds of knowing. Shakespeare, to put it crudely, "knew *how*" to write Sonnet 129: but how much did he "know *about*" his behavior in doing so? He must have known about prior specifications and the extent to which what he was writing fulfilled them. A fourth quatrain might have given him useful extra space, but he did not add one. He kept to iambic pentameter. He need not have been aware of a *double entendre,* or any other kind of word play, at the time it occurred—as anyone who has made a Freudian slip can testify—but he may have "seen" it after the fact and allowed it to stand if it pleased him. He need not have been aware of associative or assimilative influences or resulting features such as alliteration.

He need not have known about the greater part of the structural features pointed out by Jakobson and Jones. They could have played no part in the production of the primordial material (the "mutations"), and they are not likely to have played a part in the elaboration or selection of features as the poem evolved.

[10] Skinner, B. F. A lecture on "having a poem." In B. F. Skinner, *Cumulative record* (3rd ed.). New York: Appleton-Century-Crofts, 1972. Pp. 345–355.

16

Walden (One) and Walden Two

First, my credentials. I am not a Thoreau scholar, but I claim to be an amateur in the original sense of a lover. It was not love at first sight. I read excerpts from *Walden* in a course in American Literature at Hamilton College, but they were not "relevant." In those days we joined fraternities and played golf, we could not have cared less how the country was run, and as for the rest of the world we learned about that from the *National Geographic*.

When I came to Harvard for graduate study, I became interested in New England and its history, and I discovered Walden Pond. I had a bicycle and would ride out to the pond to swim, not where the bathing houses are now, but in the cove near the site of Thoreau's hut. The bottom was muddy in those days, and as I walked about in shallow water, I knew what Thoreau meant by his riparian or alluvial walks. I began to read Thoreau. I took an interest in the site; I used to go out in the late autumn to clean up after the picnickers.

Hawthorne said that Thoreau made people feel guilty about their possessions, and I know what he meant. When I got my doctor's degree, my family gave me a car, but I felt guilty about it and bought a copy of *Walden* to keep in the car to take the curse off. I made good use of it. I am almost always on time for appointments, and as Oscar Wilde once pointed out, "Promptness is the thief of time." *Walden* is an excellent book to pick up for occasional reading; even if you have time for only a few sentences, they are wonderful sentences. It does not much matter what preceded or will follow.

When I met the girl I was to marry, I took her on our first date to Walden. We had just bought a chess set in one of the shops on Beacon Hill, and on the shores of the Pond she taught me to play chess.

I moved on to the other works of Thoreau when I bought a leather-bound eleven-volume Riverside Edition. It was not complete, of course, and for many years I turned to Odell Shepard's *The Heart of Thoreau's Journals* for additional reading. I analyzed a rather long quotation from that collection in my book *Verbal Behavior*. I also bought Thoreau's translation of *The Transmigration of the Seven Brahmins*. And, oh yes, I own a Thoreau pencil—not made by Thoreau himself, I am sure, but by his family. I bought it at Goodspeed's and assume it is genuine, though I can imagine that before long someone will begin to manufacture Thoreau pencils again.

I hope this is enough to establish my status as an amateur. It may not, however, quiet the emotion some of you may have felt at my outrageous title. How could I have the nerve to put a *One* after *Walden,* even in parentheses, and set it alongside my own Utopian novel, *Walden Two?* If you found that disturbing, you were in good company. When the book appeared in 1948, *Life* magazine published a bitter editorial, denouncing it on just those grounds. *Walden Two* was called "an entirely presumptuous title." "In spirit *Walden Two* is as much like Thoreau's original *Walden* as a Quonset hut is like a comfortable and properly proportioned Cape Cod house." Further along, my book was described as "such a triumph of mortmain, or the dead hand . . . as has not been envisioned since the days of Sparta . . . If Dr. Skinner wants to imagine such a utopia, that is his privilege. But what should really be held against him is the egregious liberty he has taken with the title of Henry David Thoreau's original *Walden.* For the truth of the matter is that Thoreau's book is profoundly anti-utopian; it does not belong in the long line of antiseptic literature that began with Plato's *Republic*. Far from trying to escape into a 'brave new world,' Thoreau, the cosmic bum, set out resolutely to make the best of what he could find right around home. Where Samuel Butler traveled to Nowhere for his *Erewhon*, where Edward Bellamy marched ahead to the year 20000 A.D. for his *Looking Backward*, Thoreau set up housekeeping by the edge of a duck pond outside of his native village. As Elliot Paul has said, he 'got away from it all' by moving just a little farther from town than a good golfer could drive a ball. The lumber for Thoreau's cabin was taken from a shanty that had belonged to James Collins, an Irishman who had worked on the Fitchburg Railroad; the beans that Thoreau hoed and ate were Yankee beans, grown in recalcitrant New England soil." *Life's* complaint was summarized in this way: "Books like *Walden Two,* then, are a slur upon a name, a corruption of an impulse. All Thoreauists will properly resent them, and if Dr. Skinner comes around with any of his advice the good Thoreauist will, like Diogenes when confronted with the proffered largesse of the Macedonian king, tell the author of *Walden Two* to stand from between him and the free rays of the sun."

A few corrections, please. I submit that Thoreau would have settled for a Quonset hut. He discussed the "necessaries" of habitation (we should call them the necessities), and he designed his living quarters to satisfy them. The well-proportioned Cape Cod house is far from what he wanted. It is much more like the kind of house which, Thoreau pointed out contemptuously, cost the Concord farmer fifteen years of his life. If James Collins had left behind a small Quonset hut, I'm sure Thoreau would have been glad to move it into the woods near Walden Pond.

Nor is the community described in *Walden Two* "getting away from it all." It is one point of the book that you can have a better life here and now. You don't need to go to a Shangri-La behind high mountains, or to a new Atlantis on some hitherto undiscovered island, or move about in time to a distant past or future. You can have the kind of life you want in the present setting.

Life also called Thoreau perhaps the greatest exponent of the Yankee virtue of "use it up and make it do," and that is another point in *Walden Two*. As Thoreau said, you don't own things;

things own you. In *Walden Two* every effort is made to reduce the things needed for "the good life." I didn't realize it at the time, but there is a bonus. *Walden Two* is not only minimally consuming, it is minimally polluting.

There is no gadgetry in *Walden Two*—no computers, no tricky technical equipment. It's a simple life, rather reminiscent of an English country house in the nineteenth century, but without the servant problem. There is technology in *Walden Two*, but it is concerned with human behavior, with producing pleasant, effective personal relations—in daily life, in education, and in the production of goods.

I submit that Thoreau was a utopist in a basic sense. If you do not like the way of life that is offered you, simply build a better one. The difference is that *Walden* (One)—if you will permit me to call it that for clarity's sake—was a utopia for one. Thoreau was no hermit (he could walk into Concord—to the post office or the lyceum—whenever he felt like it), but he never came to grips with the problems which arise when people must interact with each other. *Walden Two* is an experiment in the design of a *social* environment.

And that brings me to the issue of freedom. The editorial in *Life* was contemptuous of " 'conditioning' for a 'freedom' planned long in advance according to the rigid specifications of a gang of hierarchs. In the argot of 1948, in Walden One there was simply freedom, period." But what made it possible for Thoreau to be free? Only an extraordinary set of circumstances. In the world in which he lived he was not *compelled* to do much of anything. He was free to do the things he wanted to do—to be a "self-appointed spectator at a snow storm," to anticipate nature, to begin an adventure in life starting with a vacation from toil. He could do these things by walking away from Concord and squatting on the shores of Walden Pond. But how many people can do that today?

It is easy to contrast a world in which people are controlled by other people with a world in which they seem free. Freedom from control was the dream of Jean-Jacques Rousseau, nearly a hundred years before Thoreau. By Thoreau's time the dream had seemed to come true in a successful struggle for political and religious freedom. Thoreau was opposed to political and religious despots, to armies, and to punitive education. He was opposed to punitive labor—not just slavery (to which, of course, he was actively opposed) but the slavery of the worker who commits himself to a trade or a way of life. Like Marx, who made the point at about the same time, Thoreau was opposed to wage slavery as well as the slavery which depended upon physical force. The person who works for wages is avoiding, not a flogging, but the loss of a standard of living. That is easy to demonstrate in a factory, and Marx blamed wage slavery on capital, but the principle holds for the personal entrepreneur—say, a farmer. A man may own his farm and still be a slave to it. He must plant at a certain season, and if the weather is bad within a very short season. There is no way out; he will lose the whole thing if he doesn't plant. If he has cows, there are certain times of day when they must be milked. His day is paced; he cannot do as he pleases, he must do things when he doesn't feel like doing them. As a result, Thoreau said, the farmer plows the better part of himself into the soil as compost. Any possession exacts its toil. Luxuries are a hindrance to the good life. Only leisure will show what a man is really like.

For Thoreau the alternative to the punitive sanctions of daily life seemed to be personal freedom. The feeling of freedom is associated with doing the things a person wants to do. But why does he want to do them? Thoreau never had to ask. He could also neglect other requirements of the good life. How many people today have the ethical training which gave Thoreau an interest in doing things? His fellows thought him lazy, but he knew that you "could not kill time without damaging eternity." He *employed* himself, but he did it because of his education and the ethic he had received from his culture.

He also had the benefit of the perfectionist spirit which was blowing across the land in those days. The founding of America was a unique event in the history of the world. Here was a nation which seemed to be explicitly designed in advance. Its success induced Americans to set up smaller versions of designed ways of life. More than two hundred intentional communities were founded in the United States in the nineteenth century. Perfectionist activities declined at the turn of the century, but they are beginning to return, and the change is reflected in the publishing history of *Walden Two*. In the first fourteen years, the book sold only ten thousand copies; last year it sold a quarter of a million. Something had happened in the interim. The world has come round to the necessity of doing something about the ways in which people live, and the initiative is being taken by young people. They understand what Thoreau meant when he said, "I have yet to hear the first syllable of valuable or even earnest advice from my seniors," (Unfortunately for Thoreau, he was over thirty when he said it.)

Like Thoreau, young people today are much less concerned with the purely physical conditions under which they live. Like him they avoid aversive labor, in part by cutting down on what they consume. They refuse to work hard for things which are not essential—clothing, for example. What Thoreau called the necessaries of clothing are conspicuous in Harvard Square today. Thoreau pointed out that a citizen of Concord—Emerson, say—would rather walk down the street with a broken leg than with a broken pant leg. Young people today do not mind wearing patches—they even sew patches on where there are no holes, just to prove their point. Like Thoreau, they are arguing that "Life is an experiment largely untried." Their communes are a step in the direction of new social structures. I have just read the manuscript of a charming book describing an experimental community in Virginia that is patterned after *Walden Two*. It is perhaps even closer to *Walden (One)*.

Thoreau clearly stated what must become the dominant principle in the immediate future of the world: we must cut down on the consumption of resources. It is quite impossible for our level of affluence to prevail in all parts of the world. Imagine a billion Chinese scooting around in a third of a billion cars on hundreds of millions of miles of superhighways. If I may use a horrible neologism, the rich nations must "deaffluentize." We must learn how this can be done, but Thoreau's advice is still sound: the good life is to be reached by deliberate planning.

In my contract with the publishers of *Walden Two*, the book was called *The Sun is a Morning Star*. The publishers rejected that title because another "star" book had recently been published. The phrase is from *Walden*, of course, and I worked it into the book after the title was changed. When the narrator makes his decision to go back and join Walden Two, he buys a copy of *Walden*, and as he starts his long walk back, he reads that wonderful final paragraph: "I do not say that John or Jonathan will realize all this; but such is the character of that morrow which mere lapse of time can never make to dawn. The light which puts out our eyes is darkness to us. Only that day dawns to which we are awake. There is more day to dawn. The sun is but a morning-star."

17

Freedom and Dignity
Revisited

In a famous passage in *Notes From the Underground* Dostoevski insisted that man will never admit that his behavior can be
predicted and controlled. He will "create destruction and chaos to
gain his point. And if all this could in turn be analyzed and
prevented by predicting that it would occur, then man would deliberately go mad to prove his point." Dostoevski was himself making
a prediction, of course, and it had the curious effect of cutting off
this last avenue of escape, since henceforth even deliberately going
mad could be said to have been predicted.

My critics have, nevertheless, seemed bent on proving that he
was right. Many of them have shown a taste for destruction and
chaos, some of it not far short of madness. They have resorted to
highly emotional terms, and a kind of hysterical blindness seems to
have prevented some of them from reading what I actually wrote.
An author who has been so widely misunderstood will naturally
value Dostoevski's explanation.

My argument was surely simple enough. I was not discussing
a philosophical entity called freedom but rather the behavior of

those who struggle to be free. It is part of the human genetic endowment that when a person acts in such a way as to reduce "aversive" (e.g., potentially dangerous) stimuli, he is more likely to do
so again. Thus, when other people attempt to control him through
a threat of punishment, he learns to escape from them or attack
them in order to weaken them. When he succeeds, he feels free, and
the struggle ceases. But is he really free? To say with John Stuart
Mill, that "liberty consists in doing what one desires" is to neglect
the determiners of desires. There are certain kinds of control under
which people feel perfectly free. The point has been made before,
but I was offering some further evidence recently acquired in the
experimental analysis of operant conditioning.

Such an interpretation is not metaphysics: it is a matter of
identifying certain processes in an important field of human behavior. It does not—it cannot—lead to the suppression of any freedom we have ever enjoyed. On the contrary, it suggests that there
are ways in which we could all feel freer than ever before. For
example, in spite of our supposed love of freedom, most of our
practices in government, education, psychotherapy, and industry are
still heavily punitive. People behave in given ways to avoid the
consequences of not doing so. Perhaps this means simply that the
struggle for freedom has not yet been finished, but I have argued
that the continuing use of punishment is, on the contrary, an unwanted by-product of that struggle. We refuse to accept nonpunitive
practices because they make it too clear that control is being
exerted. When we punish bad behavior, we can give the individual
credit for behaving well, but if we arrange conditions under which
he "desires" to behave well, the conditions must get the credit.

I neglected to point out that under punitive practices we even
justify behaving badly. Fortunately, this has now been done for me
by the film "A Clockwork Orange." Writing in *The New York
Review*, Christopher Ricks argues that aversion therapy takes the
protagonist Alex "beyond freedom and dignity," and he quotes
Anthony Burgess (author of the novel) in defense of the film.
"What my, and Kubrick's [director of the film] parable tries to state
is that it is preferable to have a world of violence undertaken in
full awareness—violence chosen as an act of will—than a world
conditioned to be good or harmless." Ricks says that I am one of
the few who would contest that statement. I hope there are far

more than a few. The film misrepresents the issue because the "therapy" that makes Alex good is brutally conspicuous while the conditioning that lies behind his "acts of will undertaken in full awareness" is easily missed.

The struggle for freedom has not reduced or eliminated control; it has merely corrected it. But what is good control, and who is to exert it? Either my answers to these questions have been unforgivably obscure or many of my critics have not reached the last chapters of my book. The question Who will control? is not to be answered with a proper name or by describing a kind of person (e.g., a benevolent dictator) or his qualifications (e.g., a behavioral engineer). To do so is to make the mistake of looking at the person rather than at the environment which determines his behavior. The struggle for freedom has moved slowly, and alas erratically, toward a culture in which controlling power is less and less likely to fall into the hands of individuals or groups who use it tyrannically. We have tried to construct such a culture by exerting countercontrol over those who misuse power. Countercontrol is certainly effective, but it leads at best to a kind of uneasy equilibrium. The next step can be taken only through the explicit design of a culture which goes beyond the immediate interests of controller and countercontroller.

Design for what? There is only one answer: the survival of the culture and of mankind. Survival is a difficult value (compared, say, with life, liberty, or the pursuit of happiness) because it is hard to predict the conditions a culture must meet, and we are only beginning to understand how to produce the behavior needed to meet them. Moreover, we are likely to reject survival as a value because it suggests competition with other cultures, as in social Darwinism, in which aggressive behavior is aggrandized. But other contingencies of survival are important, and the value of cooperative, supportive behavior can easily be demonstrated.

Must individual freedoms be "sacrificed" for the sake of the culture? Most of my critics contend that I am saying so, but the answer depends on how people are induced to work for the good of their culture. If they do so under a threat of punishment, then freedom (from such a threat) is sacrificed, but if they are induced to do so through positive reinforcement, their sense of freedom is enhanced. Young Chinese wear plain clothing, live in crowded quarters, eat simple diets, observe a rather puritanical sexual code and work long hours—all for the greater glory of China. Are they sacrificing freedom? They are if they are under aversive control, if they behave as they do because they will be denounced by their fellows when they behave otherwise. But if Mao succeeded in making signs of progress toward a greater China positively reinforcing, then it is possible that they feel freer, and happier, than most young Americans.

Misunderstanding no doubt arises from the word "control." Dostoevski used the metaphor of a piano key: strike it and it responds with a given tone. The metaphor was appropriate to the early reflexology of Dostoevski's time, which Pavlov's conditioned reflexes did little to change. But in operant conditioning a stimulus merely alters the likelihood that a response will be emitted. Good examples are to be found in verbal behavior. A verbal response is very different from the knee-jerk elicited by a tap on the patellar tendon. What a speaker says is determined in part by the current listener, in part by the recent verbal stimuli he has heard or seen, in part by a nonverbal setting, and in large part of course by his history as listener and speaker. These variables can be sorted out by identifying well-established behavioral processes.

There was an excellent example of the probabilistic control exerted by a verbal stimulus at a recent symposium at Yale University organized to discuss *Beyond Freedom and Dignity*. On the second evening, several students brought in a large banner reading "Remember the Air War," which they hung from the balcony. It could not be seen by many in the audience, but it confronted the five panelists on the platform throughout the evening. It had a predictable effect: Everyone of us mentioned the war in Vietnam at some point in his discussion and the last speaker, Sir Denis Brogan, put aside his manuscript and spoke only of the war.

That was good behavioral engineering. We should learn to live with it.

18

Freedom, at Last,
From the Burden of Taxation

New Hampshire was first to have a lottery, perhaps because it enjoys a unique opportunity to induce visitors to support its government. But other states soon found that their own citizens preferred voluntary support to taxation and lotteries quickly spread. One can only applaud the zeal and ingenuity with which they have been managed. Madison Avenue has done its best. Lotteries are advertised in airports and buses, in newspapers and magazines, on television and the radio. Newspapers cooperate in publicizing the thrills of winning. When it was discovered that some people could not wait for a deferred drawing, instant lotteries were invented. All this is admirable, and we are grateful for the resulting reduction in taxes, but I wish to point out that an important resource has been overlooked—our schools.

People are not born gamblers. They become gamblers when exposed to certain sequences of lucky hits. Why should our schools not be used to expose everyone to such sequences? The necessary behavioral technology is at hand. All that is needed is a system of lotteries extending from kindergarten through high school in which the odds are at first highly favorable but grow steadily worse until, upon graduation, the student will find the standard lottery with its meager odds irresistible. I propose something like the following.

In kindergarten the tickets will cost a penny and prizes will be of the order of a dollar, with a grand prize now and then of five dollars. The odds will be extremely favorable; at this stage the state will lose money, but of course the amounts involved will be trivial. In the first three grades tickets will cost a nickel, prizes will be in the five-dollar range, except for a grand prize of, say, fifty dollars, and almost all the money collected will be returned in prizes. The grand prizes will be awarded in ceremonies in the several schools. In the next three grades tickets will cost a dime, the prizes will range from ten to fifteen dollars with a grand prize of the order of a hundred or two hundred dollars. The state will return approximately 85% of the money collected, and the grand prizes will be awarded in city-wide ceremonies. In junior high school tickets will cost a quarter, prizes will be on the order of twenty-five dollars, with a grand prize of perhaps five hundred. The state will return about 60% of the money it collects and winners will be announced on local television. Finally, in high school, tickets will cost fifty cents, prizes will be of the order of fifty dollars, with a grand prize of a thousand, and at this point the state will pay back about 50% of what it takes. The grand prize will be awarded in a ceremony on state-wide television with an admired figure partici-pating.

Since practically all the expenses of administration will be borne by the schools, the entire operation will be much more profitable than the regular lottery. The result will be a yearly crop of high school graduates who will continue to buy lottery tickets for the rest of their lives, even though the lotteries continue to pay back no more than 40% or 45% of the amount wagered.

In other words our schools will be used to create vast numbers of young people who come on the market each year as dedicated (should we care if psychiatrists call them pathological?) gamblers. The effect of one year's crop may not be felt, but by the end of five years I estimate that sales taxes can be abolished and that after twenty-five years (and we must look ahead!) there will be absolutely no need for state income taxes. After that the states will be able to help cities reduce their taxes on real estate.

When programs of this sort have been set up in all the states, the full potential of our schools will be realized. The entire population above the age of six will know the joy and excitement of weekly (or daily!) drawings. A huge national lottery will be inevitable and Federal income taxes abolished. My guess is that the Pentagon will run its own lottery and thus escape forever from the annoyance of those appeals to Congress. I do not think I am being unduly sanguine in looking forward to the day when the support of our government—in city, state and nation—will be entirely voluntary.

Economists will point out that money spent for lottery tickets will not be spent for goods and services and that business will suffer. But the loss will be more than offset by the absence of taxes and by the money won. The only important economic change will be a very considerable increase in the consumption of luxury goods and services. The rich, released from the burden of taxation, will be able to spend much more on luxuries and so will the big winners —only one further proof of the virtue of voluntary action in the support of a society of free and happy people.

Acknowledgments

The chapters of this book were presented and published as indicated below. Permission to republish is gratefully acknowledged.

1. Presented: American Psychological Association, Washington, D.C., September, 1976. Published: *Psychology Today*, September, 1977.
2. Presented: Walgreen Conference on Education for Human Understanding, University of Michigan, April, 1973. Published: *Impact*, 1973, *3*(1), 5–12.
3. Presented: A symposium on "The Control of Behavior: Legal, Scientific, and Moral Dilemmas," Reed College, March, 1975. Published: *Criminal Law Bulletin*, 1975, *11*, 623–636, and in *The Humanist*, January/February 1976.
4. Presented: Humanist Society, San Francisco, May, 1972. Published: *The Humanist*, July/August 1972.
5. A preface to a new printing of *Walden Two* (Macmillan, New York, 1976).
6. Presented as a Herbert Spencer Lecture, Oxford University, November, 1973. Published: In R. Harré (Ed.), *Problems of scientific revolution: Progress and obstacles to progress in the sciences*, (Oxford: Clarendon Press, 1975), and *American Psychologist*, 1975, *30*, 42–49.
7. Presented as a Phi Beta Kappa Oration at Harvard University, June, 1976. Published: *Human Nature*, February, 1978.
8. Presented: Inter-American Society of Psychology, Miami, Florida, December, 1975. Published: *Behaviorism*, 1977.

9. Presented at a conference at the New York Academy of Sciences on "The Roots of American Psychology," April, 1976. Published as "The Experimental Analysis of Operant Behavior" in R. W. Rieber and K. Salzinger (Eds.), *The roots of American psychology: Historical influences and implications for the future* (*Annals of the New York Academy of Sciences,* Vol. 291), New York: New York Academy of Sciences, 1977, pp. 374–385.

10. Published: In C. E. Thoresen (Ed.), *Behavior modification in education* (Chicago: National Society for the Study of Education, 1973, pp. 446–456).

11. Presented: New York University, October 19, 1972. Published: *New York University Education Quarterly,* Winter 1973, *4,* 2–6.

12. Published: *Daedalus,* 1974, *103,* 196–202.

13. Published in a memorial volume in honor of Jerzy Konorski: *Acta Neurobiologiae Experimentalis,* 1975, *35,* 409–415, and *Journal of the Experimental Analysis of Behavior,* 1975, *24,* 117–120.

14. Published in a festschrift for Sidney Bijou: B. C. Etzel, J. M. LeBlanc, and D. M. Baer (Eds.), *New developments in behavioral psychology: Theory, method, and application* (Hillsdale, New Jersey: Lawrence Erlbaum Associates, 1977, pp. 3–6) and in *The Humanist,* May/June 1977.

15. Published in a festschrift for I. A. Richards: R. Brower, H. Vendler, and J. Hollander (Eds.), *I. A. Richards: Essays in his honor* (New York: Oxford University Press, 1973, pp. 199–209).

16. Presented: Thoreau Society, Concord, Massachusetts, June, 1972. Published: *The Thoreau Society Bulletin,* Winter, 1973, *122,* 1–3.

17. Published: *New York Times,* August 11, 1972, p. 29.

18. Published: *New York Times,* July 26, 1977.

Robert Epstein has improved the consistency of many technical expressions and in other ways given much appreciated help. I also thank M. J. Willard for assistance in the preparation of the manuscript.

Index

Abstraction, 98
Abulia, 38
Accountability, 132
Acedia, 38
Adaptation, 18
Adrian, E. D., 114
Advice, 108
Affluence, 13
Agencies, 9, 15
Aggression, 38
Agriculture, 84
Aid, 47
Alienation, 12, 38, 90
Allen, Layman, 138
Alliteration, 182, 184
American Civil Liberties Union, 43
Anatomy, 69
Anthropology, 59, 91
Apathy, 38
Applied analysis of behavior, 41, 45
Aquinas, Saint Thomas, 51
Arctic tern, 167
Aristotle, 77
Assertion, 179
Association, 97, 110
Assonance, 182
Attitude, 48, 89
Attneave, Fred, 104
Audiovisual devices, 130

Aversive control, 3, 7, 11, 22, 135, 143, 152
Awareness, 111

Bacon, Francis, 77
Bats, 164
Beauty, 91
Behavioral engineering, 57
Behavioral sciences, *Chapter 7*
Behaviorism, *Chapter 4*, 72, 111
Behavior modification, 10, 15, 40f., 45, 82
Behavior therapy, 121
Bell, Sir Charles, 76
Bellamy, Edward, 190
Bentham, Jeremy, 81
Bernard, Claude, 79
Bigness, 62
Books, 154
Boredom, 38
Braverman, 38
Bridgman, P. W., 117
Brogan, Sir Denis, 198
Buddha, 66
Burgess, Anthony, 196
Bussey Institute, 164
Butler, Samuel, 190

Calvin, John, 68, 82
Carr, A., 165, 168
Cassandra, 17
Castell, A., 57
Catholicism, 53
Causality, 172
Chained responses, 21
China, 31, 65, 92
Classroom management, 135
Clockwork Orange, 196
Club of Rome, 29
Cognitive psychology, *Chapter 8*, 74
Cohen, H. J., 43, 62
Coincidence, *Chapter 14*
Coleman, P. J., 165, 168
Collins, James, 190
Comenius, 35
Communes, 193
Communication, 35
Communism, 65
Computer, 75, 106
Concept, 99
Conditional reinforcers, 22f.
Conditioned reflexes, 113
Confidence, 86
Confucius, 66
Conscience, 53
Consciousness, 90, 111
Consequences, 19
Contingencies of survival, 167
Contingency-shaped behavior, 12
Contrived reinforcers, 145
Control, 14, 197
Controlling agencies, 24
Corporal punishment, 143
Countercontrol, 8, 27
Covert behavior, 100
Creative behavior, 150
Credit, 78
Crime, 62, 101
Crozier, W. J., 114
Culture, 9, 14, 34, 53, 125, 132, 158, 197
Cybernetics, 74

D'Alembert Jean le Rond, 81f.
Darwin, Charles, 18, 76
Davis, Hallowell, 114
Delinquency, 62
Democracy, *Chapter 1*
Denmark, 44
Density of meaning, 180
Descartes, René, 51
Development, 99
Dewey, John, 144
Dews, Peter, 123
Diderot, Denis, 81f.
Dignity, *Chapter 17*, 79
Diogenes, 190
Directions, 108
Discovery, 131, 150
Doomsday prophecies, 17

Dostoevski, 195, 198
Dualism, 49
Dyer, Henry, 133

Economic incentives, 24
Economics, 59
Economist, 13
Education, 64, 129
Educational contingencies, 24
Educational philosophy, 152
Educational policy, 147
Education for life, 159
Edwards, Jonathan, 102
Enlightenment, 66, 81
Environment, 85, 104
Epistemology, 124
Ervin Committee Report, 45f.
Escape, 6, 25
Eskimos, 44
Ethical self-management, 150
Ethics, 46, 52, 158
Ethics of helping people, *Chapter 3*
Ethology, 82
Evolution of cultural practices, 24, 78
Examinations, 137, 150
Existentialism, 26, 48, 54, 150
Experimental analysis of behavior,
    Chapter 9, 82, 134
Exteroception, 50
Extinction, 116

Face to face control, 9f.
Feeling of freedom, 31
Feelings, 71, 85, 91, 101
Feigl, Herbert, 57
Ferster, C. B., 122
Filipczak, J., 43, 62
Final causes, 18
Forbes, Alexander, 114
Fourth estate, 28
Fraser, Ronald, 168
Free and happy student, *Chapter 11*
Freedom, *Chapter 17*, 6, 25, 31f., 63, 79,
    143, 191
Freedom to have a future, *Chapter 2*
Free school, 26, 146
Freud, Sigmund, 51, 59, 90, 187
Froebel, Friedrich Wilhelm August,
    140
Fuller, Paul, 121
Future, *Chapter 2*, 144f., 150

Gambling, 199
Genetic endowment, 32
Goodman, Paul, 130, 140
Greeks, 104, 109
Greenland, 44

Hamilton College, 188
Happiness, 32, 61, 93
Harvard University, 188
Hawthorne, Nathaniel, 188
Health, 64
Hedonism, 19
Heilbroner, R., 38
Helping, *Chapter 3*
Heron, W. J., 123
Hippy culture, 26
Hobbes, Thomas, 77
Holland, J. G., 121
Holt, John, 130, 140
Homeric Greek, 74
Homing, 164
Hubler, Edward, 177
Human behavior and democracy, *Chapter 1*
Humanism, *Chapter 4*
Humanistic psychology, 26, 54

Idea, 99
Idols of the School, 151
Illich, Ivan, 131, 140
Images, 107
Imprinting, 124
Individual, 54, 80
Individual pacing, 155
Indochina, 47
Industry, 38
Information theory, 74
Inside information, 73
Institutional care, 40
Intellectual self-management, 150, 173
Intelligence, 133
Intention, 48, 102, 179, 184
International Peace Research Association, 91
Interoception, 50
Introspection, 51, 72, 111
Iowa, 42
Imitation, 22
Immediate gratification, 32
Incentives, 27
Intermittent reinforcement, 21
Intervention, 15
Iran, 87

Jakobson, Roman, 176, 179, 182f., 185f.
James, William, 51
Jefferson, Thomas, 7
Jensen, B., 44
Jesus, 66
Jones, 176, 179, 182f., 185f.
Jouvé, Jean Pierre, 182
Julesz, Bela, 105

Kant, Immanuel, 51

Keller, F. S., 136, 138, 146, 156
Koestler, Arthur, 171
Knowing, 48, 73, 104
Knowledge, 105
Konorski, Jerzy, 119
Kozol, Jonathan, 130, 140

LaFarge Center, 53
Langer, Suzanne, 101
La Rochefoucauld, François, Duc de, 70
Law of Effect, 19, 35, 115
Laws, 108
Learning, 130
Leisure, 63
Lenin, 65
Lewis, Arthur, 89
License, 80
Life magazine, 189
Lilienthal, D. E., 87
Limits to Growth, 29
Lincoln, A., 3
Lindsley, Ogden R., 121
Linguistic competence, 110
Linguists, 122
Locke, J., 7, 51, 77
Loeb, Jacques, 113
London *Times*, 88
Lotteries, *Chapter 18*
Lucero, R. J., 42
Luck, 175

Mach, Ernst, 117
Machiavelli, Niccolò, 14
Macmillan Company, 57
Magnus, Rudolph, 114, 119
Malthus, T. R., 56
Man, 73
Mao Tse-tung, 32, 198
Marx, Karl, 12, 34, 39, 66, 81, 192
Mathematical models, 74
Maxims, 108
McNeill, W., 95
Meaning, *Chapter 15*
Measurement, 149
Medicine, 77
Memory, 76
Mental apparatus, 110
Mental hospitals, 41
Michotte, A., 173
Middle Ages, 100
Migration of birds, 166
Mill, J. S., 77, 196
Miller, S., 119
Mind, 100, 107
Minnesota, 123
Molière, 110
Money, 23, 46
Montessori, 140, 143

Morals, 52, 158
Moynihan, D. P., 88
Myth, 174

National Research Council, 58
National Training School for Boys, 43
Natural Selection, 18f., 76
Neill, A. S., 140
Nervous system, 123
New Hampshire, 199
New York Times, 13
Noncontingent reinforcers, 12f., 36
Nozick, Robert, 47

Objectives of teaching, 134, 146
Onians, R. B., 73
Operant behavior, 103, 120
Operant conditioning, 19, 42, 172
Order, 179
Orr, R. T., 167
Osterwald, H., 166

Parts of speech, 179
Pasteur, Louis, 79
Paul, Elliot, 190
Pavlov, I. P., 74, 97, 113ff., 119, 198
Pavlovian conditioning, 10, 40
Pedagogy, 130
Perfectionism, 192
Permissiveness, 6
Personalized system of instruction, 136
Pestalozzi, 140
Phenomenology, 26, 48, 54
Philosophy, 113
Phylogenic behavior, *Chapter 13*
Physiology, 49, 69, 81, 111, 125
Piaget, Jean, 109
Plato, 51, 73, 77, 190
Poincaré, Henri, 117
Political action, 66
Political science, 59
Pollution, 61
Popper, Karl, 98
Positive reinforcement, 4f., 11, 40, 145
Possession of facts, 105
Practice, 108
Press, 28
Prisoners, 43
Probability, 36
Programmed contingencies, 13, 41
Programmed instruction, 121, 135, 146, 156
Progress, 39, 53, 133
Propositions, 104
Proprioception, 50
Prosthetic environment, 41
Protestant work-ethic, 61
Proverbs, 108
PSI, 136

Psycholinguists, 122
Psychology, 59
Psychopharmacology, 123
Purpose, 19, 102
Pursuit of happiness, 7

Ransome, John Crowe, 179
Rapaport, Anatole, 103
Rate of eating, 115
Rate of responding, 116
Real world, 131, 144, 152
Rehabilitation, 43
Respondent conditioning, 21
Reston, James, 13
Revival of Learning, 66
Rewards, 35
Richards, I. A., 186f.
Ricks, Christopher, 196
Rights, 40f.
Robertson, J. M., 177
Rogers, Carl, 36, 125, 130, 144
Romans, 77
Rousseau, Jean-Jacques, 131, 140, 191
Royal Society of Arts, 86
Rules, 12, 108
Russell, Bertrand, 113, 117
Russia, 65, 83, 89

St. Paul, 36
Salmon, 167
Scherber, J., 42
Schmidt, J., 168
Scholastics, 77
Schumacher, E. F., 60
Science of behavior, *Chapter 6*
Scientific American, 27
Scientific creativity, 110
Scientists, 29
Selection, 163
Self-actualization, 54
Self-control, 52
Self-knowledge, 50, 52, 111
Sense of self, 52
Sense of time, 100
Service, Elman, 65
Sexual identity, 99
Shaping behavior, *Chapter 13*, 120, 163, 168
Sherrington, C. S., 74, 114, 116, 118f.
Silberman, Charles, 130, 140
Social Darwinism 30
Social environment, 8, 83
Socialism, 65
Social psychology, 91
Sociology, 59, 91
Sonnet, 180
Spontaneous generation, 79
State of mind, 48
Statistics, 174
Stimulus control, 169

Stomach memory, 20
Storage, 106, 125
Stream of consciousness, 111
Strength of behavior, 38
Structuralism, *Chapter 15,* 14, 20, 48, 54
Summerhill, 130, 141
Superstition, 20, 153, 172
Survival, 50, 53, 126
Susceptibility to reinforcement, 21
Swinburne, Algernon Charles, 183ff.
Systems analysis, 74

Teachers, 28
Television, 130
Tennessee Valley Authority, 87
Textbook, 154
Theory of knowledge, 124
Therapy, 197
Third world farmers, 84
Thoreau, Henry David, 64, 188ff.
Thorndike, Edward L., 19, 35, 115f., 119, 130
Thought, 100
Tinbergen, N., 101
Tokens, 41f., 145
Tolman, E. C., 117f.
Topography of behavior, 169
Turtles, 164
Tyler, A. F., 57

UNESCO, 91
United States, 31, 47, 83
Utilitarianism, 35, 46, 154

Vail, D. J., 42
Values, 52, 92
Verbal behavior, 109, 139

Waddington, C. H., 101
Walden, Chapter 16, 64
Walden Pond, 188
Walden Two, Chapter 5, Chapter 16, 29
War, 91
Warnings, 108
Warren, Robert Penn, 57
Watson, J. B., 113
Wegener, A., 168
Welfare, 13, 64
Will, 100, 102
William James Lectures, 122
Wolfson, A., 166ff.
Woodworth, R. L., 116, 118
Word association, 98
Wordsworth, William, 183
Work, 39
Wundt, Wilhelm Max, 51

Zaharoff, Sir Basil, 47